LIBRARY OF THE EARLY CIVILIZATIONS
EDITED BY PROFESSOR STUART PIGGOTT

The Royal Hordes

THE ROY

NOMAD PEOPLES OF

McGRAW-HILL BOOK

AL HORDES

THE STEPPES

E. D. Phillips

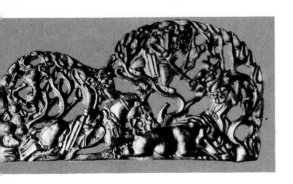

COMPANY · NEW YORK

DESIGNED AND PRODUCED BY THAMES AND HUDSON

CONTENTS

GENERAL EDITOR'S PREFACE

The settled, urban, civilizations of antiquity were always uneasily aware that beyond the boundaries of their control there were other peoples, with other modes of life, who constituted a potential threat to ordered peace. Such peoples might not even be agriculturalists, and all the more footloose and dangerous for that. Around 2000 BC Mesopotamian civilization was being threatened by barbarian nomads raiding into settled territories, among them those who appear as the Amorites in Biblical tradition—'the Amorite who knows not grain' wrote the scribes of the Kingdom of Akkad: 'a host whose onslaught was like a hurricane, a people who had never known a city'.

People who did not cultivate fields or live in towns were always there in ancient Europe and Asia on the edges of the peasant or urban world, ready to make themselves felt over sometimes vast and improbable distances. Writing of the mid-thirteenth century AD Edward Gibbon spoke of the alarming conquests of the nomads at that time: 'The Latin world was darkened by this cloud of savage hostility . . . it might be apprehended that the shepherds of Scythia would extinguish her cities, her arts, and all the institutions of civil society.' And, with his characteristic flair for vivid and significant detail he noted how fear of the oriental invasions had disrupted the activities of the Baltic fishing fleets: 'It is whimsical enough' he added in a footnote 'that the orders of a Mongol khan, who reigned on the borders of China, should have lowered the price of herrings in the English market.'

Whimsical perhaps, but as the great historian acutely perceived the nomad world was one of huge extent, and events at one end of it could have unexpected repercussions at the other. And more than that, Gibbon realized that the nomads of antiquity were powers to be reckoned with by the historian, and not to be relegated to a marginal obscurity.

Their geography is that of the open grasslands of the steppe country, which like the prairies of North America afforded natural pasture for the local herds of wild game: in Eurasia the horse was to be the most significant animal of the world beyond that of the ancient agricultural communities. But with the initial domestication among these earliest farmers of sheep and goats, and later of cattle, the great grazing grounds of the steppe were available for pastoralists and peasants.

In such an environment pastoralism of some kind, not necessarily initially wholly nomadic, would early be developed as a viable economy. The nomadic quality becomes the more insistent as the economy is developed the more fully to exploit the grazing resources of the country in terms of more than one type of domesticated animal. 'We must not,' Sir Ellis Minns reminded us 'regard nomadism as a mere stage on the way from food-collecting to agriculture. When completely developed, it is a highly specialized mode of life enabling man to utilize vast tracts in which continuous settlement, whether pastoral or agricultural, is impossible.' Such nomads 'most move regularly between wide areas which afford fodder during the spring and early summer and the restricted pastures in which they can tide over the winter'. Developing this theme, Richard Beardsley has added: 'The true pastoral nomad technology (and I believe this is the proper term) includes a complex of animals rather than a single species, balanced in terms of grazing characteristics to utilize all the grass cover of each locality. Cattle, horses and camels graze well on long grass: sheep and goats crop close.'

It is within the area of the South Russian steppe, and at a period before 2000 BC, that the evidence of archaeology and linguistics combine to suggest that we have the homeland of those speaking the language or group of closely related dialects ancestral to the great Indo-European family, represented by such languages as Greek and Latin, Celtic and Sanskrit, and the Slav group. The earliest documentary evidence for any members of this family is that relating to the Hittites, who were establishing their power in Asia Minor by about 1900 BC; by inference the dialects ancestral to Greek must have been introduced into what became their homeland at much the same time. Celtic or its immediate linguistic ancestor may well have been transmitted to central and northern Europe equally early, though the speakers of Sanskrit do not seem to have conquered the north-west of the Indian sub-continent until comparatively late in the second millennium BC. So far as barbarian Europe is concerned it is possible that an element of pastoralism also permeated the ancient world of sedentary Neolithic peasants with the earliest speakers of Indo-European tongues, to remain as an economy alternative to agriculture up to the time when it is reflected in the earliest hero-tales of Celtic Ireland, composed before the fifth century AD but representing even earlier conditions.

But of all the nomad peoples of the Steppes in antiquity it is the Scythians, and their successor-tribes of Sarmatians and the like, who have won the most enduring fame. The Greeks may have encountered them in trading ventures as early as the eighth century, BC, and with the founding of the Black Sea colonies from about 600, began to know them as a curious and barbarian people and, as John Boardman remarks, rather as Red Indians once appeared to us – 'a remote race of dusky warriors who wore long trousers and funny hats, were phenomenal bowmen, and scalped their enemies'. Peisistratos seems to have formed a corps of Scythian archers in the Athenian army in the later sixth century, and the Scyths soon acquired a reputation not only as bowmen, but as Noble Savages; just in fact as South Sea Islanders and American Indians played this role in eighteenth-century England with (in both instances) invented speeches of high moral tone being put into their mouths when appropriate.

Archaeology not only confirms, but greatly amplifies the picture of Herodotus and other writers. We today can appreciate the qualities in Scythian art in a manner impossible to sensibilities formed in the classical mould, and can find in it, and all the related arts of the Northern Nomads, something immediate and exciting, disturbingly allusive and haunting. To its making there went many traditions, some striking roots back into the ancient hunting and fishing peoples of Eurasia, others linked with the schools of metal-work which had grown up on the edge of the steppe around the Caucasus from before 2000 BC.

The Scythians were the eastern neighbours of the Celts, another people with a great barbarian art style, not unrelated in its feeling. The Scyths could and did raid into east Europe, and into the fringes of the newly forming Celtic world of the sixth century BC while perhaps no better witness of the widespread striking power of this warlike tribe could be found than the bronze arrowheads of Scythian type found in the destruction-levels of hill-forts in Poland on the one hand, and on the other in the mud walls of the Urartian palace of Karmir Blur in Russian Armenia, two thousand miles away to the south-east.

STUART PIGGOTT

INTRODUCTION

When Professor Stuart Piggott first asked me to contribute a chapter on the nomads to *The Dawn of Civilization*, I was glad of the opportunity of trying to present the earlier phases of their long and complicated history as an interconnected whole. I regretted then that there was not space to carry my account down on a uniform scale to the desired conclusion, the end of the Indo-European period on the northern steppes. But in this extended version I have made an attempt to do just this.

The reader should find a historical framework, with maps and tables added, which will accommodate and roughly locate any important phase or event in the history of nomadism from its neolithic or chalcolithic origins in the third millennium BC down to the moment when the entire northern steppe was dominated by the swiftly moving hordes and empires of Turkish or kindred peoples. The same framework is intended to give a background for all the archaeological discoveries mentioned or illustrated.

Though I have aimed at producing an intelligible whole, I have naturally given prominence to the grander and more elaborate tombs and finds. But it must not be forgotten that innumerable simpler burials have been found, which in any exhaustive account would take up most of the space. The treasures of the ruling chiefs show a mode of life which was at once barbarous and sophisticated in a manner hardly found among settled peoples. But other barbarians left something similar in their graves, when without being nomads they were yet wanderers and fighters in many countries. The Scythian and Sarmatian chiefs in this aspect are not unlike the more powerful chiefs of the Celts or the more successful Vikings of later ages.

In art the distinctive contribution of the nomads is their Animal Style, unsurpassed in vigour and unique in its conventions and distortions. It was the creation of the Iranian nomads under influences which are discussed, and it faded away among later nomad peoples, though they lived the same life in the same environment. This fact, as well as those of ethnology and philology, makes it appropriate for the present study to end with the Huns.

The nomads are of special interest because their way of life was an alternative to civilization, not a mere absence of it. It was once fashionable to trace three stages in human culture: hunting and fishing, pastoral life, and finally settled farming, which culminated in civilization. We believe now that nomadism is much more likely to have originated from mixed farming by way of specialized stockbreeding, diverging in this way from that other line of development which led through intensive agriculture to an economy capable of supporting cities. The evidence also shows that completely specialized nomadism, in particular mounted nomadism, is considerably younger than urban life, more than ever if that includes the life of pre-pottery Jericho and any such other walled settlements that may be discovered. Nomadism may have proved to be a blind alley in human progress, but its importance for the fate of empires and for military history at large cannot be ignored.

My debt to the writings of many scholars of various kinds will be obvious from the bibliography, but among those that I have met I must record my gratitude to Dr R. D. Barnett of the Department of Western Asiatic Antiquities at the British Museum, who for a number of years has answered my queries in this field or indicated where answers might be found. I must also acknowledge, in this version as in the earlier one, the expert help of members of the firm of Thames & Hudson in getting and preparing the illustrations which are so important a feature of such books as this.

E. D. P.

CHAPTER ONE

The Nomad Peoples of the Steppes

The Steppes

The northern steppes, in their immense extent from Hungary to Manchuria, form a peculiar region of the world. In South Russia and western Siberia they are more like the prairies of North America, and well suited to agriculture or to pasturage. But in other areas, particularly in Central Asia and farther east, they are now desert, not so different from the Sahara, Arabia and the Near East, which have also been the home of peoples with the nomadic mode of life who have made their mark on history.

The whole region between the northern forests and the great mountain zone which divides northern from southern Asia falls into two halves, a western and an eastern, which for the period here under consideration have different histories.

Ill. 1

The western half begins with the Hungarian plain between the Balkans and the Carpathians. It extends through parts of Rumania and Bulgaria to South Russia and to East Russia between the Caucasus mountains and the Ural forests. It continues through southern Siberia and the region of Kazakhstan, north of the Persian plateau, to a mountain barrier consisting of the Pamir,

1 The Eurasian Steppes during the Neolithic and Early Metal Ages before the Mounted Nomads

HER   C U L T U R E S

PEOPLES

YENISEI

LOWER TUNGUSKA

LENA

AMUR

TOI TRIBES

Yablonovy Mts

OB

IRTYSH

Reindeer

Minusinsk

Sayan Mts

LAKE
BAIKAL

Khingan
Mts

ost

O C U L T U R E

AFANASIEVO CULTURE

KARASUK CULTURE

M O N G O L I A N
T R I B E S

MANCHURIA

STAN

LAKE
BALKASH

Z U N G A R I A

Altai Mts

KARASUK MIGRATION?

GOBI DESERT

JEHOL

SEMIRECHIE

Tien Shan Mts

NEOLITHIC
SPREAD?

TARIM

HWANG-HO

ORDOS
DESERT

LUNG
SHAN
CULTURE

Pamir   TARIM

T A N

NEOLITHIC

Anyang

YANG
SHAO
CULTURE

Karakoram
Mts

Nan Shan

SHANG CHINA

Kwen Lun Mts

T I B E T

C H I N A

Himalaya Mts

the western Tien Shan, the smaller ranges east of Lake Balkash, and the Altai mountains bordering on Outer Mongolia. The eastern half beyond the Pamir can again be divided into two areas of steppe, a southern one stretching north of Tibet and south of the Tien Shan through the Tarim basin to north-west China and Mongolia, and a northern part, running north of the Tien Shan likewise to Mongolia. In Mongolia the two parts join and continue, with the Ordos desert attached on the south, through the Gobi desert between China and the eastern Altai to the Khingan mountains and to Manchuria beyond them. The eastern half is higher and harsher in climate, contains far more desert, and is sharply marked off from the mountains and from the cultivated lands of China. The northern and southern boundaries of the steppes come closest to one another in the region of Zungaria, north of Sinkiang, which has often been a decisive territory for the passage of wandering nomad hordes.

East of Zungaria and far to the north and south in eastern Asia the dominant types of man from the beginning of our period have been of the mongoloid type, as represented today by the Chinese. They originated perhaps in the Gobi region before or during the last glaciation, perhaps 50,000–20,000 years ago. In the northern forests they spread westward to the shores of the Baltic, where their presence has been traced by anthropologists (by means of characteristic skull-types) in the hunter-fisher population of the Neolithic period, about 2000 BC. On the western half of the steppes the earliest population belonged to the white races; mongoloids hardly appear there before the Hunnish movement into Central Asia during the last centuries BC. But white nomads were known on the north-west border of China during the first millennium BC and later left descendants among the Mongols themselves.

The course of events on the northern steppes during the period of growth of the great civilizations is a vast and vague subject, far less compact than the development of any more settled communities. It shows neither its full importance nor any degree of unity until the end, when the nomad societies, the distinctive product of the steppes, begin to make their contribution to world history. By 1000 BC the ancient civilizations of the first generation had largely run their course and left their permanent mark on mankind. The nomad societies, on the other hand, had at that time no long history behind them, but were destined during the next two thousand years and more to intervene catastrophically in the affairs of many civilizations. To trace their origin is thus a historical task of the highest interest, and only in our time has it become possible to do so in the light of scientific excavations.

European knowledge of the steppes in ancient times began with the study of the Greek descriptions of the Scythians given in the *History* of Herodotus (written in the fifth century BC), and in the medical essay, *Airs, Waters and Places*, of about the same date and attributed to Hippocrates. These could be supplemented from the later historians who deal with the Huns, and from such European writers as Carpini, Rubruquis and Marco Polo, who described the Tartars in the Middle Ages. From the eighteenth century onward the Greek sources began to be tested by excavation of the great mounds of the Russian Steppe, which revealed burials corresponding closely with those mentioned by Herodotus, and described later in this survey. At the same time archaeological exploration of the Near East brought to light Assyrian and other records, in which information was found of nomad invasions, confirming and supplementing Herodotus. In the Far East, Chinese records have yielded some evidence concerning the nomads early in the first millennium BC. Meanwhile prehistoric archaeology has been continued in Russian territories by Soviet scholars, who have added greatly to our knowledge and finally provided a general framework for the entire history of the ancient nomads. Nomadism as a developed way of life, however, arose relatively late from a background of more or less settled agricultural communities, and it is to the origins of these that we must first turn in order to be able to understand the later developments which led to the rise of nomadism.

The Beginnings

In Siberia and Mongolia the Palaeolithic (Old Stone Age) traditions lingered long, and even at a period contemporary with the beginnings of civilization in Western Asia, man was still a hunter without the opportunity for agriculture, using spears and arrows tipped with bone, various bone tools, rounded stone axes, and a crude pottery. In the remoter parts around Lake Baikal and in Manchuria, skeletons of the same period are found with remains that show only the primitive hunting and fishing economy of late palaeolithic type. Farther south stone tools of the so-called 'microlithic' type and arrowheads have been found in the Gobi and Ordos regions. Before the pottery-making phase this culture extended southward through Central Asia and the Aral region to the Indian Ocean. It represents an advance on the Palaeolithic, and had evidently spread from the south-west through the eastern half of the steppes, probably in moister conditions than those that now prevail. The steppes even then appear as a corridor allowing the spread of population and techniques over great distances to the east. In the west these early periods are already beginning to be dominated by stone-using cultures involving animal husbandry and grain cultivation, described below.

Agriculture and Herding

The most plausible theory for the origin of herding is that it arose from agriculture in places where the wild animals grew accustomed to feeding on plants cultivated by men. This would most naturally happen in countries of little rainfall, where the best watered ground near springs or rivers would often be occupied by human cultivators. Though they would not be welcome at first, the animals under stress of hunger would be persistent visitors and become familiar with the sight of man. These would be the best conditions for catching them alive and keeping them for later eating. The value of females for milk would soon be obvious, and eventually also the usefulness of the larger and stronger animals for work.

The earliest known agriculture, at any rate of cereals, began as we have seen in Western Asia, before the seventh millennium BC, precisely in these dry conditions, and on occasion (as at Jericho) round about sources of water. As early as the fifth millennium (and perhaps before) sheep, goats and cattle, and later even the onager or wild ass, appear to have been tamed, to judge from bones on the sites. If stock-breeding arose as part of the first neolithic culture in Western Asia, we have also a readier explanation for the development of specialized herding on its southern fringe in Arabia and North Africa, where the known history of nomadism begins earlier. It is most important for our purpose that though the onager and the ass are native to the Near East, the horse is not, so that horsebreeding cannot have originated there.

During the fourth and third millennia BC peoples with subsistence based on mixed farming, making pottery and using stone tools, began to spread towards the northern steppes. One route along which these new techniques of living spread lay north-eastward through Iran to Turkestan, where near Merv, the settlement of Anau had a long history. Another route ran north-westward through southern Asia Minor, across the Aegean to Greece, and so through the Balkans to the Danube valley and South Russia. It is less easy to trace a direct northward spread through the difficult country of Armenia and the Caucasus. From South Russia, where the Tripolye culture was in existence probably from the middle of the fourth millennium, and from Central Asia, neolithic cultures apparently reached North China and neighbouring regions.

The neolithic basis assumed for stockbreeding is thus likely to have existed at suitable places throughout the northern steppes at least from the fourth millennium onwards, and this could have developed on the fringes of cultivation into specialized herding. It is clear that in suitable conditions this could arise anywhere from the neolithic mixed economy, and also from any similar economy in the early stages of the use of metal, as in the Bronze and Early Iron Ages.

The Tripolye Culture (c. 3500–1900 ? BC)

This culture is important not only because of its early date, but because of its difference from succeeding cultures, which were nomadic. It takes its name from Tripolye, near Kiev, where it was first excavated, and was the product of communities that carried on mixed farming of the neolithic pattern on the fertile wind-blown soil or loess, stretching from the lower Danube round the eastern end of the Carpathians and across Bessarabia and the Ukraine as far as the Dniepr, and for some distance beyond. The painted pottery, clay models of houses and clay figurines made by the Tripolye people show their affinity with the neolithic peoples of the Balkans. Four main stages can be recognized (referred to here as Phases I–IV), between approximate limits of 3500 and 1900 BC; the earlier date is rather hypothetical but is supported by recent C-14 tests. Nearly all the details known are derived from settlements and not from burials.

Life was based on the cultivation of wheats, barley and millet, and on the breeding of cattle, goats, sheep and pigs, the last unsuited to a nomadic existence and native to wooded country. The bones of horses occur at all levels, and the tame horses of this culture are probably the earliest in history. They were apparently at first kept for meat, but later are likely to have carried and drawn loads. Wheeled vehicles are not known from these sites, but there are clay models of sledges. The camel was known towards the end of the Tripolye phase, no doubt as an import from the east. In the refuse of food, the percentage of game-bones declines steadily. Fishing is attested by fish-hooks of bone or copper from the earliest sites, and small perforated pieces of clay are probably net-sinkers. Copper was first used for fish-hooks, rings, bangles and beads, and later for axes, adzes, picks and broad daggers with a central rib. There is no sign yet of the plough drawn by animals.

Ill. 2

The settlements were generally in defensible positions on spurs of loess above river valleys. The most representative sites are in the region of wooded steppe, not on the barer steppe or near the coast. At Vladimirovka on the Bug the largest village known contained (in Phase III) as many as two hundred houses in five concentric circles. Their sites are represented by platforms of baked clay resulting from the burning and collapse of walls and floors. Post-holes for timber frames define rectangular floors varying between 7 × 4 metres and 27 × 6·5 metres. The walls were of wattle and clay or of compacted earth, coloured over, and the roofs probably of thatch. A middle-sized house (Phase II) contained two separate rooms, each with a clay oven 2 metres square, set against the wall, while the largest known house at Vladimirovka

Ill. 3

contained five rooms, four with one oven and the fifth with two. The floors are of well smoothed and hard baked clay, and on the underside show the imprint of close-set timbers that supported them. It is not certain whether there was empty space under the timbers, as has sometimes been claimed; they may simply have rested on the earth. These floors were proof against damp, rodents and insects.

Among the fixtures, the clay ovens were constructed on frames of saplings, which left their impression on the inner surface. The frames would no doubt perish with continual heating, but by the same process the clay would

2 A reconstruction of life among the people of the Tripolye culture, based on the remains found at Kolomishchina in the Ukraine dating from the late fourth and early third millennia BC. Huts, crops, harvesting women with flint-bladed sickles, pigs and cattle in the distance among the huts, and men carrying home a slaughtered deer are shown. The position of the village on high ground by the river is indicated in the background

3 The Tripolyans lived in houses of clay and wattle. These can be reconstructed from platforms of clay, which show the impress of floor-beams, and from other remains. The clay was baked hard when the walls and floor were burned. The cut-away drawing shows the reconstruction of a two-room house at Vladimirovka. Against the wall each room had a clay oven, which would serve for heating as well as cooking. The clover-shaped platform, sometimes found adorned with paint or with engraved lines, has been interpreted as an altar. The roof would be of thatch and the floor of clay or trodden earth resting on close-set timbers

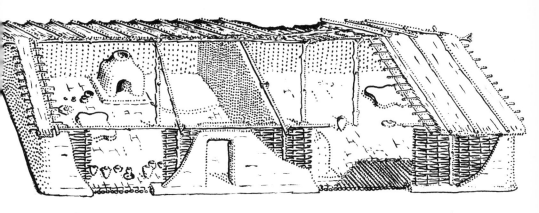

4 Pottery models of Tripolyan houses show a gabled roof and designs on the walls like those on pottery itself

become nearly as hard as earthenware. Apart from baking bread and cooking, the ovens no doubt served in winter as stoves to warm the houses. Beside them were wide raised benches of baked clay, which could be used as shelves, and would also have been convenient for sitting and sleeping. Near the centre of the floor in every room was a low clay platform about 0·25 metres high, shaped like a cross when viewed from above, and adorned with engraved lines or with paint. These have been interpreted as altars for offerings. The cross-shape is stout and rounded, and recalls the shapes of altars known from Minoan sites on Crete, such as Mallia.

Though the 'altars' themselves have been found only at Vladimirovka, models of them occur elsewhere as parts of complete clay model huts, also belonging to this period. A very remarkable round model hut from Popudnia stands on short legs, which again suggests that the original building was raised on piles, and has a sort of porch. It contains an altar, an oven, three vessels on a bench, and two small female figurines, one of a woman grinding with a stone quern by the porch, and another, seated by the oven, who may be the protecting goddess of the house. This seeming dolls' house no doubt had a religious or magical purpose, and is now exceedingly helpful to archaeologists.

Ovens, benches, and altars were apparently the only fixtures. The movable objects were, typically, querns for grinding grain; jars for holding liquids, flour and seeds, other pottery, tools as described, needles, spindle-whorls and a great number of clay statuettes, nearly all of them

Ill. 4

Ill. 5

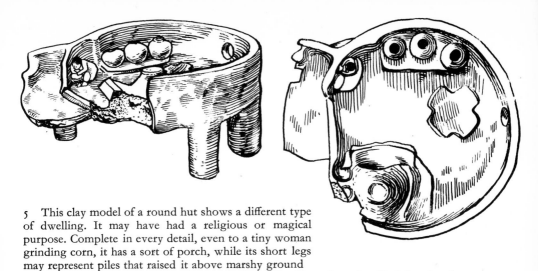

5 This clay model of a round hut shows a different type of dwelling. It may have had a religious or magical purpose. Complete in every detail, even to a tiny woman grinding corn, it has a sort of porch, while its short legs may represent piles that raised it above marshy ground

6 The head of this clay figurine from Vladimirovka shows the style of hairdressing for women

female. The statuettes are usually found near the ovens or the altars. Many of them were no doubt used for the rites of an agricultural religion. The commoner type of figurine is nude, and may represent the mother-goddess, as in the Balkans, the Aegean, and Western Asia. These may have been dressed for ritual occasions. Others seem to represent women, and have painted on them belts, which could have held up skirts, a sort of bodice, and a style of hair-dressing that suggests a chignon. Traces of plant fibres and wool from excavations confirm the existence of clothing of these materials. The figurines show that the feminine influence was strong. Though the remains include battle-axes, it is not likely that war was common or serious among such communities.

Ordinary domestic pottery of a plain kind was made, probably by the women, from stocks of prepared clay, such as were discovered in some houses. Professionally made pottery was red or orange, with elaborate, often spiral, designs painted on in darker colours, sometimes over a white slip. This was fired in vertical kilns such as one whose remains were found at Erösd in Transylvania, stacked with vases.

7 Such elaborate pots as this, with spiral designs in purplish brown on a yellow background, were professionally made in kilns, such as the one found at Erösd, and were not domestic ware

The last stages of the village however show that settled life was increasingly abandoned. Large settlements disappeared, agriculture declined into second place as a source of livelihood, and the painted pottery gave way to another type. The Tripolye culture must have been broken up by immigrants who had a pastoral culture and a different structure of society.

Farther east, in Siberia there is still no evidence for any settled culture as old as the Tripolye, but there, and on the drier steppes, any remains would have been much more easily destroyed by cattle and winds. Yet it is of some significance that the Chinese Yang Shao culture of painted pottery occupied similar sites on loess terraces overlooking rivers, and in the Aral region the neolithic hunters and fishers of Kelteminar used a red painted pottery.

CHAPTER TWO

The Rise of Pastoral Societies

Thus far we have followed the slow spread over the northern steppes of settled agricultural communities derived from those of Western Asia. We now come to the beginning of pastoral societies on the northern steppes, which at their furthest development were as different from the settled cultures of the Near East as were the nomads of the southern deserts. In the west this process is also connected with another of special significance, the rise and spread of the peoples speaking Indo-European languages, to whom many of the northern nomads belonged.

The evidence for these earliest pastoralists comes almost wholly from graves, often under mounds or barrows forming groups or cemeteries, the monuments of these ancient peoples, visible even today on the wide steppe-land. The disentangling of the different cultural traditions over the vast area where the various groups had once moved with their flocks and herds is not an easy task, but what can be deduced is set out below.

The Usatovo Culture

As early as Phase III of the Tripolye Culture in South Russia, the earliest known form of a different society was growing up on its fringes toward the Black Sea and the Caucasus. At Usatovo near Odessa remains were found

of a society, probably with a more marked social strati-
fication, which made greater use of metal and buried its
chiefs under conspicuous mounds or barrows in cemeteries. The bodies were interred in a contracted position
on one side, or on their backs, in a central shaft encircled
by slabs set on edge. Slaves or dependants were killed
and buried in accessory graves before the earth was
heaped over the whole, and bones of animals and statuettes
were buried in separate pits. Flat graves elsewhere, perhaps those of cultivators, consisted of shallow pits under
flat slabs. Degenerate pottery and figurines of Tripolye
style were found in both kinds of burial, and also a coarse
ware bearing cord-impressions which some have thought
characteristic of the early Indo-European peoples.
Animal bones were very numerous and represented far
more horses and far fewer pigs than Tripolye remains.
The new type of pottery and selection of animal bones
represent a pastoral element. Copper, in the form of
daggers, flat axes, quadrangular awls and spiral rings, is
much more abundant; some of the spirals are also of
silver. The type of copper object distributed along the
coast suggests a source overseas.

The Ochre-Grave Cultures

Farther south and east remains are found of other cultures that have something in common with that of
Usatovo but no Tripolye basis. They are distinguished
usually by their barrow-graves, and by the habit of
covering their dead with red ochre. Some of the 'ochre-
graves', as they are called, are covered with long mounds
and contain skeletons reddened with ochre arranged in
groups. At Mariupol, on the Sea of Azov, 120 adults
and 6 children were buried in a long communal grave; at
Volnishki near Dniepropetrovsk 130 skeletons were
buried together and at Nalchik in North Caucasia 130
contracted skeletons were found, both under long

mounds. A knobbed stone mace-head at Mariupol and copper rings, probably worn as hair ornaments, and carnelian beads at Nalchik show trading connections with the Near East, where such things could be obtained.

These various forms of burial are almost the only evidence we have of these peoples. Russian archaeologists have classified them as the cultures of shaft-graves, pit-graves and timber-graves, though the pit-graves (or catacomb-graves) are confined to the coast of the Black Sea and the basin of the Don. During this period, from the end of the third millennium and through the second, the richly furnished burials of the chieftains of the Caucasian Copper Age appear, again under large barrows. Finds from domestic sites of the period, of pit-graves under round barrows (burials, as the name implies, in a simple pit in the ground), show that cattle, sheep and goats were bred and millet cultivated. In a barrow at Storozhevaya Mogila near Dniepropetrovsk remains of a wooden cart with two solid wheels, used as a hearse, were found, which shows that wheeled vehicles had begun to be used on the Pontic Steppe by the end of the third millennium, as also at Budakalasz in Hungary, where a grave contained a clay model of a four-wheeled cart. At Ul in the Caucasus a clay model of a covered waggon may be dated about 1800 BC. Developed nomadism on the northern steppes was scarcely possible without waggons to transport families and their belongings.

Afanasievo

Eastward in Siberia and Inner Asia during the same period developments are illustrated from the best explored region, the basin of the Upper Yenisei above the zone of forests.

Here remains representing communities living from perhaps 3000 to 1700 BC have been named by arch-aeologists the Afanasievo phase, after the locality of

Afanasievaya Gora. We only know these peoples' graves, in the form of oval or rectangular trenches covered with stone slabs. Some burials are communal, some individual. The skeletons, as in the earliest herdsmen's graves on the Dniepr, are tall and long-headed, and in the Altai region, to which this culture also extends, some skulls are of the so-called Cro-Magnon type, long but with short broad faces. Again, as in South Russia, the dead are buried on their backs or on their sides in contracted position, and covered with ochre. In the Altai region the graves are in chambers roofed with stone slabs or tree trunks and covered with small barrows. Apart from tools of bone or antler, and bones of cattle, sheep and horses, these graves contain simple red pots, mostly with conical bases, recalling pottery styles from Transcaucasia, Persia and Transcaspia, and also copper plates, needles and spiral ornaments. Cultural links therefore are with the west and south-west among these earliest stockbreeders of Siberia. They were quite different from the neolithic mongoloids of which archaeological traces have been found to the north-east.

The Andronovo Culture

The next stage, dated provisionally from 1700 B C onward, is named after Andronovo on the Yenisei. It is best represented in the Minusinsk depression, an enclave of grassland in the forest, and in various forms covers the western Altai, the Semirechie, the Aral region, and Kazakhstan. It is known chiefly from burial grounds varying between three and fifty graves. The graves are marked with stone slabs or by small barrows surrounded with circles of stones. The burial chambers are lined with stone or tree trunks, and the dead usually lie in a bent position, but some were cremated. The racial type of the skeletons is again European, now for the first time with an admixture of the round-headed white race from the

Pamir. These people made large flat-bottomed vases of a smooth brown pottery ornamented with triangles, diamonds, swastikas and other geometrical designs, or with meanders. Arrowheads are often of bone but sometimes of copper, like the occasional axes, knives, daggers and sickles, and moulds for casting these have been found. Gold is very common, and is used for covering plates of copper or bronze.

Remains of the horse and camel show that stockbreeding was important, but the copper sickles and stone hoes also indicate agriculture. One wealthy grave contained horses, probably to be ridden by the privileged dead. Some settlements have been found with large houses and an open space by the village, believed to be for laying out loaves. There is evidence everywhere of a tendency to form settled communities, except in eastern Kazakhstan. Russian prehistorians regard the phase as the greatest development of mixed economy in Siberia and Central Asia, though much later than the rather similar economy of Tripolye in the west. In western Siberia, Kazakhstan and the Aral region it lasts for a long time. In the Yenisei basin and in the Altai by 1100 BC or a little later a new culture appears, named after Karasuk in Minusinsk, which has important links with China.

The South Russian Region (2500–1000 BC)

From these communities of the third and second millennium BC, whose material equipment as known from their graves does not provide us with anything more than the rather humdrum products of peasant activity and skills, we can turn to look once again in the South Russian region, this time to the country north of the Caucasus, between the Black Sea and the Caspian. Here we encounter barrow burials again, but with a rich and varied equipment buried with the dead which make them merit the title of Royal Tombs.

A development in the prestige and wealth of the people of the ochre-graves must have begun towards the end of the third millennium in northern Caucasia, where wealthy chiefs' tombs show clear links with the Near East, in the form of luxury goods imported or copied from foreign originals. These tombs are situated in the basin of the Kuban River, on the northern side of the Caucasus. The burials resemble that already described at Nalchik, but are much richer and contain far fewer bodies. They are in fact the first princely burials, or Royal Tombs, of a kind recurring at times for centuries afterwards among the pastoral warriors of the steppes, and show a much sharper distinction of rank between chiefs and subjects, such as arose when pastoral societies became wealthy.

The Maikop Burial

The most famous of these burials, and apparently the earliest (probably about 2300 B C), is that at Maikop on the Byelaya. Under a mound 10·65 metres high, at the level of the ground and within a ring of vertical slabs of limestone, was the main burial in what had been a rectangular wooden chamber 5·33 metres × 3·73 metres. Before all the wood had rotted and the earth fallen in from above, the grave had been walled and roofed with beams and its floor laid with broken stones; outside, a large wooden structure had been built enclosing it. The inner space had been divided into a northern and a southern compartment, and the northern compartment again into a western and an eastern half.

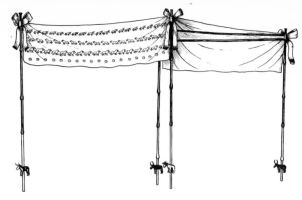

8, 9 Two gold bands with gold rosettes (*Ill. 8*, left) were probably set on a tiara or cap of cloth or felt worn by the chief buried at Maikop. *Ill. 9*, a reconstruction of the canopy as it was when it covered the chieftain's bier, showing poles, bull figures, crosspieces, cloth with gold figures sewn on to it, and ribbons

In the middle of the southern compartment lay a man's skeleton with knees drawn up and head to the south, as in most of these burials, and thickly covered with ochre. The body was strewn with gold ornaments and beside it lay rods of gold and silver tubing with small figures of bulls in gold or silver. There were also beads of gold, turquoise and carnelian with the body, gold studs, rings of gold wire, and pierced disks of silver and gold. Vessels of gold or silver, or of stone adorned with these metals, stood along the eastern and western walls, some crushed by the earth on the collapse of the burial chamber.

Ill. 10

From this collection of treasures about the body the burial could be reconstructed as it would have appeared when the tomb was closed and the great mound piled on the timber structures. The chieftain was probably wrapped in coloured robes, such as those later to be mentioned from Novosvobodnaya, and wore on his head a tiara of cloth or felt ornamented in front with two golden diadems, studded with golden rosettes, that were found near it. The rods, each made of three fitted sections of gold or silver tubing, seem to have been the frame of a processional canopy held over the waggon or bier by four bearers. As carried in the procession, these four rods had been uprights, held at the bottom by bearers. Their lowest sections ran down through the bull-figures and projected a hand's breadth below, so that the figures would have rested on the bearers' hands, facing forwards. Through slits in the top sections, which were crowned with gold or silver caps, also found, ribbons had been

Ill. 8

Ill. 9

Ill. 10

10 One of the gold figures of bulls which formed part of the canopy's frame. The bull's back is pierced by the hole for one of the poles. The breed appears to be short-legged with very long and wide-set horns, like some that appear in Elamite and Sumerian art

passed to hold on the canopy. Two other rods without bulls or caps had been cross-pieces, perhaps fastened with ribbons, stretching from front to back.

In the tomb, the canopy that once covered this frame had been laid as a pall over the dead. Sixty-eight gold plaques in two sizes, representing lions, and nineteen similar ones representing bulls, all of them pierced with a few holes round the edges, lay among the bones. These had been sewn to the canopy, probably to front and rear flaps only, since more would have been needed for the whole cloth. The gold disks had also been sewn on, while the beads had belonged to necklaces or bracelets.

Ills. 11, 12

Among the vessels were two egg-shaped silver vases with necks. On one is incised a most remarkable design – nothing less than a complicated landscape. In the back-

11, 12 Two silver vases from the Maikop burial. *Ill.* *11* has what appear to be figures of panthers wearing collars: another link with regions south of the Caucasus. *Ill.* *12* has a complicated landscape. A similar element of landscape appears in some early Babylonian and Egyptian scenes of animals. The bull emulates in its relief the solid figure of *Ill.* *10*. The wild boar and the bear climbing the tree seem to be local subjects

ground is a jagged range of mountains, interrupted by two palm-trees and a bear reared up between them; in the foreground two streams flow down into a round lake. Across this scene walk two processions of animals: in one a bull, a wild steppe horse, and a lion with a bird of prey on its back, while another bull faces the opposite way; in the other a boar, a tiger perhaps, and two wild mouflon sheep. The second vessel shows in procession a bull, a mouflon, panthers apparently with collars, and a duck-like bird.

Among weapons were an axe-adze, a straight-bladed axe and a cross-bladed adze, all of copper, the last two of Mesopotamian type, and evidently the symbols of power and authority of the chieftain in life. Flint arrowheads lay by the body.

Of the other two chambers, the eastern one contained the skeleton of a woman with earrings of gold wire, beads of gold and carnelian, and vessels of copper, and the western a man's skeleton with beads and a large earthenware jar. These are likely to have been servants, put to death to accompany their master.

Other Burials

Ill. 13

The burial at Maikop, though most remarkable and exciting, is not unique. Two graves discovered under great mounds at Tsarskaya, now Novosvobodnaya, were similarly those of chieftains or members of princely classes. These differed from that of Maikop in having chambers which were of stone and not wood (like the 'dolmens' of the northern Caucasus mentioned below), but contained similar weapons. One was gabled, like a miniature house, the other was flat-roofed, and both had two compartments, the larger in each case containing the body. Ochre was spread over the bodies and in one case even on a wall of the chamber. Among the weapons were curious socketed fork-heads of copper, rather like pitchforks, but with their points bent into hooks; one was even adorned with human figures. In the second grave the skeleton was still wrapped in a black fur coat with the hair outside and a silver collar; under this was a cloak of camel's wool with black stripes, and under that again a linen garment with a purplish-red border. These precious surviving fragments show how much we have lost of the craftsmanship in furs and textiles of these peoples.

These princely burials resemble in many respects others south of the Caucasus at Alaca Hüyük. Their contents recall the treasures at Troy II in Asia Minor and the finds at Hissar in Iran. All are related to Mesopotamian royal burials in their conception and in the style of some of their contents, particularly the bronze

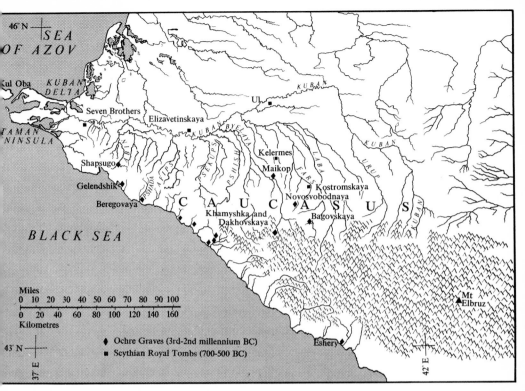

13 The map shows Maikop and other sites of early ochre graves; also sites of the North Caucasian dolmens of the Bronze Age

weapons. The design of landscape and animals on one of the Maikop vases has general affinities with Near Eastern work, and the lions, tigers, and panthers as subjects point in the same direction. It is likely that the vases and plaques are imports, or the work of a craftsman from Western Asia. No burials equalling these in splendour are known on the steppe in the Kuban region or near it until the Scythian period, more than a millennium later, when contact with the Near East was again close. The semi-precious stones used for beads include carnelians from India or Iran, lazurite from Central Asia, and meerschaum from Anatolia.

14 A decorated slab, pierced with a 'porthole', from a dolmen near Storozhevaya, North Caucasia. Of the human figures, one man holds a pitcher, another a plough, the third is perhaps a woman

In this region archaeologists have determined a sequence of cultures from the early second millennium BC onwards, named Nalchik, Kuban, and Kuban-Terek, of which the last extends right across the Caucasian Steppe. Later in the Kuban stage (after 1500 BC) the connection with the Near East was broken off, and the peoples of these regions were thrown upon their own resources in metallurgy. They made connections instead with the Danubian region and the Urals for new supplies, apparently not yet knowing those of Transcaucasia.

Ill. 15

In the North Caucasus stone-built tombs known as 'dolmens' were being built at this time. They are usually built in the form of a square or oblong stone cist, roofed with a similar slab and pierced through one wall with a hole for offerings. But some are boxes hollowed out of one massive rock. Their connections seem to be Asiatic rather than European or West Mediterranean. The best known are those of Gelendshik, Beregovaya, Dakhov-skaya and Storozhevaya, and of the avenue at Novo-svobodnaya. They contained copper or bronze weapons, such as spearheads, axes and daggers, and also arrowheads and small blades of flint.

Ill. 14

Transcaucasia (Second Millennium BC)

Transcaucasian cultures of the Bronze Age show more affinity with the Hittite and Hurrian world of that time. The most notable remains are those found in the forty-

15 A stone burial chamber with 'porthole' at Gelendshik, North Caucasia

two barrows of Trialeti in the valley of the Khram, west of Tiflis in Georgia.

These were dated by the excavators to the eighteenth century B C, but others place them later in the sixteenth and fifteenth. Each contained one body only, that of the local chief, as was shown by the richness of the funeral furniture. Under the mounds were clay platforms, or in other cases pits 7 or 9 metres deep, sometimes with stone walls. The remains of the dead were cremated; one set of bones rested on a massive four-wheeled wooden carriage. They were surrounded by the bones of edible animals, tame and wild. There were no remains of horses, no objects of iron and almost no weapons of metal. Of the pottery, some was painted with spirals that recall the decorations of Mycenaean pottery.

Some metal objects were of special interest. A bronze spearhead from the fifteenth barrow had a socket ringed with silver. Spearheads of exactly this type are otherwise known only from Greek sites of the Mycenaean shaft-grave period and slightly later, and from places under Mycenaean influence, such as the sixth city of Troy and the site of ancient Ugarit in Syria. The same barrow contained a bronze cauldron with a movable handle. In the eighth were disks of gold with repoussé decoration comparable to pendants from the tombs of Mycenae. Such finds naturally bring to mind the Greek legend of the Argonauts who sailed to Colchis. Most curious of all

37

16, 17 A silver goblet (*Ill. 16*) from the fifth barrow at Trialeti has heads on the human figures which are puzzling. Some scholars have even thought that they are ill-done human heads, but wolf's head masks are most likely and the figures apparently have tails; this would at any rate suit the fauna of a wooded region. *Ill. 17*, a gold cup from the seventeenth barrow at Trialeti, is of unalloyed metal, and decorated with filigree work and mounted stones.

Ill. 16

is a silver goblet from the fifth barrow, decorated with embossed figures in two registers. In the lower register is a procession of deer, in the upper a religious procession of twenty-three human figures, carrying goblets and apparently wearing hollow heads or masks of boars, moves towards a figure seated on a throne beside a sacred tree, with two altars and sacrificial animals near by. The deer have analogies in Caucasia and Anatolia, while the upturned shoes of the human figures have a Hittite look.

Ill. 17

From the seventeenth barrow came richly decorated gold goblets and a gold-handled silver bucket decorated with crowding figures of deer; also a silver dagger and silver pins with gold heads.

Such burials must represent a long tradition. They are later than the barrow of Maikop, and their affinities seem to lie farther west, but they too are evidence of Near Eastern influence in the Caucasus.

CHAPTER THREE

The Indo-European Migrations

The First Indo-European Migrations
(c. 1900–1000 B C)

During the long period of rising pastoral societies the
Indo-European peoples, who all show traces of such a
phase in their history, must first have come into prominence. Attempts have been made to equate linguistics
and archaeology north of the Black Sea and the Caucasus,
and to suggest that the corded pottery and the battle-axes
of stone or metal that spread through eastern Europe at
this time, particularly on the fringes of the old Tripolye
and Danubian cultures, were made by speakers of Indo-
European tongues. It is likely that the Indo-European
languages arose on the Pontic and Caucasian Steppes, not
far from Anatolia, where Hittite and related languages of
the Hittite Empire have left written traces beginning
early in the second millennium.

Though the route by which the Hittites entered Anatolia cannot yet be traced archaeologically, it is a reason-
able guess that they arrived about 1900 B C by way of the
Caucasus. The same route was probably taken by the
ruling element among the people known as the Kassites
in the Zagros mountains, who seem to have had Indo-
European names. It was also no doubt followed by a
much stronger group, the Aryans, later of India and Iran,

Ill. 18

18 The steppes and neighbouring regions during the rise of mounted nomadism and

during the Scythic period

evidence of whose language appears early in the second millennium south-east of the Hittites in the country of the Hurrians, originally a Caucasian people. People with Indo-European names ruled the Mitannian kingdom in northern Iraq and Syria in the middle of the second millennium. Others passed on through Iran to found the Sanskrit-speaking Aryan society of India. Corded pottery found in the stone cist-graves of Kayakent near Derbent has been claimed as evidence that the Aryans passed the Caucasus by this route along the Caspian coast. Some Indo-European names of Mitannian kings appear with Caucasian suffixes in Hittite texts. The name of the ancient Sindians of the Kuban delta may be the Sanskrit *sindhava*, 'men of the river'. It is suggested that these Indo-Europeans remained in their old home when the majority passed southward, to arrive eventually on the banks of another river that they likewise called Sindhu and we call the Indus.

Another movement of Indo-Europeans passed southward to settle in Iran, after which country the whole group to which they belong has since been named Iranian. Those who settled in Iran were the ancestors of the Medes and Persians, who created civilized empires in the Near East. Those of the same group who remained north of the Caucasus became mounted nomads, the Iranians of the steppes, with whom we shall be much more concerned. Other Indo-Europeans to take up mounted nomadism were some of the Thracians and also the Tocharians.

The Conditions of Nomadism (1): Waggons and Chariots

In spite of the important part played in the development of a characteristic economy by the pastoral peoples so far described, the peoples of the steppes did not exert their greatest effect on the outside world until the rise of mounted nomadism, which is the culmination of ancient life on the steppes. But the change follows closely on the full development of an earlier use of the horse in war for drawing the light chariot with spoked wheels.

In Mesopotamia the Sumerians had by 3000 B C or so converted the waggon to military use as a heavy war-car, with solid wheels, drawn by onagers. The horse appears to have been introduced for drawing a new light kind of war-chariot with spoked wheels by the Hurrians of North Syria, already mentioned, or rather by their Indo-European rulers. It is a plausible suggestion that the Indo-Europeans brought the horse to south of the Caucasus early in the second millennium, and that the Hurrians as their allies and subjects developed the light chariot in this suitably timbered region for the faster and more manageable animal. The war-chariot as a revolutionary weapon invented on the edge of Near Eastern civilization became a decisive factor in warfare in the Near East itself, in Europe, and also, as is now apparent, so far away as China.

How it reached China is not certain, but it appears in the armies of the later rulers of the Shang Dynasty at Anyang in the twelfth century B C. Traces of chariots have been found in Shang tombs, and the current early form of the Chinese script contains a sign for chariot.

The Karasuk Culture (c. 1000 B C)

The population of the Minusinsk region now shows a great increase, and physical remains appear of a mongoloid type, but usually with some special traits not found in the peoples of the Siberian forests, but belonging to the northern borders of China. The skeletons are slight and the skulls small, low, and narrow in the face. The animal bones in the graves show an increase of sheep-breeding, but the many large pots suitable for grain storage suggest that agriculture continued. A monumental

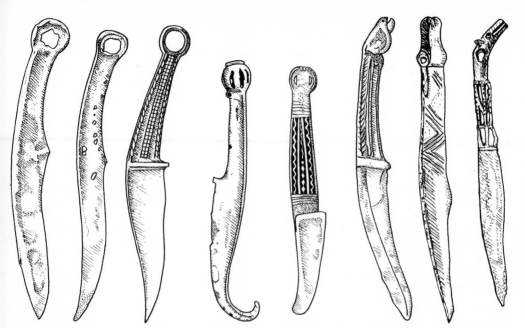

19 Three groups of bronze knives dated from 1300 BC onward suggest influence from China through Mongolia on the Karasuk culture of Minusinsk on the Upper Yenisei. On the left are ring-headed knives; on the right, more elaborate forms with animal heads. In each group the first is from Anyang, the second from the Ordos and the third (at right and left only) from Minusinsk

stone upright or stele near Znamenka shows a covered waggon drawn by a single horse. The camel was used extensively but there appears to be no reason for considering these people nomadic, in spite of the evidence for sheepbreeding.

The graves are shallow stone cists, and contain pottery with round or pointed bottoms, not flat bottoms as in Andronovo graves. The vessels are finely made, smooth and thin-walled, suggesting Chinese influence. But the strongest links with China are in metal-work, particularly in the types of bronze knife which occur also at Anyang, on the Ordos Steppe, and in Mongolia. The knives are sometimes S-shaped with points curved back, but more commonly inward curving, with the handles terminating in rings, in animal heads, or in jingles. Sometimes the animal terminals are not merely heads, but standing figures, single or in rows. Knives and daggers with such

Ill. 19

handles suggest a Chinese element in the famous Animal Style which, as we shall see, is characteristic of the mounted nomads in the next phase, and is their notable contribution to the world's decorative art.

Peculiar to this Karasuk culture are the curious stone stelae shaped like sabres and carved on their sides with human faces, on which a pattern of radiating lines is again attributed to Chinese influence. Some form of the Karasuk culture is also found in the region of Semirechie and in the Tien Shan. But farther west Kazakhstan and Siberia west of the Altai are still occupied by a late form of the Andronovo culture until 800 BC.

The Second Indo-European Migrations (c. 900 BC)

Both these groups of peoples were next to be disturbed and overrun from the west by a new immigration of peoples of European type. It has been suggested that the beginning of this process may have been a movement of tribes from South Russia to the north-western border of China. The objects found in the area include axes, picks, daggers, belt clasps, crossed tubes for harness, metal buttons, buckets, and such decorative motifs as wolf's teeth, characteristic of the Late Bronze and Early Iron Age peoples of Eastern Europe, including Caucasia. Perhaps their carriers were Indo-Europeans, now riders, including bands of those peoples known to the classical writers as Cimmerians, Thracians, Illyrians and maybe even early Germans. There may also have been among them the ancestors of the Tocharian people of the Tarim basin, who spoke an Indo-European language and were part of the white-skinned Yueh Chi horde mentioned later by Chinese sources. This movement would have taken place after 900 BC, and would be part of the last phase of the great secondary expansion of Indo-European peoples from Eastern and Central Europe which began about 1200 BC.

20 A Karasuk stele from Tasmin, Minusinsk. The human face shown here is evidently not one of the more mongoloid types

45

The Conditions of Nomadism (2): Riding

Thus for the opening of the next era in the history of the steppes we are brought back once more to South Russia and the Caucasus, where mounted fighters had begun to be decisive in battle and to create societies of mounted nomads. For this step not only the earlier taming of the horse for work, but probably also its use with chariots by the Aryans in the Near East was a necessary preparation. There is evidence that riding of other animals was known earlier in the Near East than on the steppes, but riding did not become common for civil or for military purposes until the horse had been introduced in convenient numbers by the Aryans, at first for driving.

Evidence for riding becomes more abundant late in the second millennium. For example a Hurrian relief from Tell Halaf of the fifteenth or fourteenth century B C shows a mounted warrior. A Kassite seal of the thirteenth century from Luristan appears to show a mounted archer in fantastic form. Mycenaean potsherds from Ras Shamra (Ugarit) in Syria of the fourteenth or thirteenth century may show riders in formation. In the eleventh century Nebuchadnezzar I of Babylon mentions riding horses. At the other end of Asia, a Shang grave near the site of Anyang, dated to the eleventh century, contained a single man's skeleton buried with weapons and jade ornaments and the skeleton of a single horse and of a dog. He appears to have been a foreign rider, a hunter and warrior, and perhaps a nomad. Riding in Shang China, if it was introduced from the west, raises the same problems of transmission as chariot-driving. But cavalry are not mentioned in Chinese sources for centuries after this.

On this evidence it appears that regular riding was coming into fashion in the Near East at any rate after the fourteenth century B C, and that it spread thence through the mountain zone to the steppes. But neither this, nor even cavalry, is mounted nomadism. According to some,

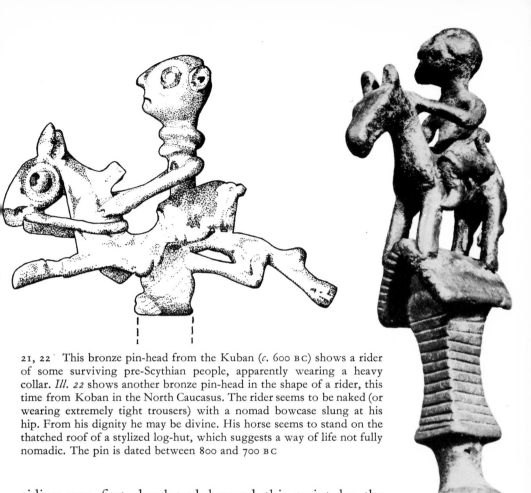

21, 22 This bronze pin-head from the Kuban (*c.* 600 BC) shows a rider of some surviving pre-Scythian people, apparently wearing a heavy collar. *Ill. 22* shows another bronze pin-head in the shape of a rider, this time from Koban in the North Caucasus. The rider seems to be naked (or wearing extremely tight trousers) with a nomad bowcase slung at his hip. From his dignity he may be divine. His horse seems to stand on the thatched roof of a stylized log-hut, which suggests a way of life not fully nomadic. The pin is dated between 800 and 700 BC

Ills. 21, 22

riding was first developed beyond this point by the peoples, partly Aryan and partly of older local origin, of Transcaucasia and northern Iran. Mounted warriors went not only southward from this region into the Near East as conquerors and mercenaries, but northward as plunderers against the pastoral peoples of the steppes, who did not yet ride as a general habit. The pastoral peoples could make no effective resistance to the attacks of cavalry, and were bound either to yield their flocks and herds as plunder, and so lose their livelihood, or to submit to the rule of their mounted enemies, paying tribute in cattle. If they wished to resist they were obliged to become mounted fighters themselves. In either case there would come into being communities of mounted warriors who controlled many subject tribes and large flocks and herds on the steppes. The more these took to the open steppes, the more purely nomadic they would become. Since the new form of military power depended on great herds of horses with enormous requirements in good fresh pasture, military needs would be added to the motives for conquering more areas of fertile steppe.

Impact of the Nomads on Previous Cultures

In this way the first of a long succession of nomad empires would be formed. The process has been compared to the known spread of mounted fighting among the Indians of the American prairies, once these had learned the art from the Spaniards in the south. The Pontic-Tocharian migration described above might have been the beginning of this advance. These communities of riders spread through the territories of the unwarlike late Andronovo and Karasuk cultures of mixed farmers and herders. Recent evidence favours the theory that these mounted warriors were the first Indo-Europeans to reach Siberia and Inner Asia.

There is nothing in common between the remains of the Andronovo culture and those of the first Aryans in Iran. The 'timber-grave' culture of the Pontic Steppe (see above, p. 28) just before the Scythian period is also different from the Andronovo. On the northern edge of Kazakhstan in the centre of the Andronovo culture, Andronovo pottery is succeeded suddenly by another style, a change that should be the result of political and military events. The Andronovo culture persists only in fortified places on the wooded edge of the steppes, where the agricultural tradition continues west of the Altai. It is likely that the people there first fell under the rule of the nomad Sarmatians, related to and contemporary with the Scythians, and finally suffered a military disaster. In Minusinsk the white element in the population (perceptible in skull types) is suddenly reinforced from no nearby source. Near Karaganda at Dyndybay forms of pottery like those of Andronovo exist side by side with forms which are new to the Asiatic steppe and like those of northern Caucasia and South Russia. In the Aral region the Iranian movement comes northward from Iran itself. On the borders of China there were movements of nomads in the Chou period (first millennium B C), and Chinese sources mention their red hair and green eyes.

Other Simple Cultures in Contact with the Nomads (First Millennium B C)

Some other non-nomadic cultures of limited extent now deserve a brief mention for their contact with growing or developed nomadism during the next period. They belong to the forested steppe of European Russia and were perhaps created by the ancestors of some of the Finno-Ugrian peoples known later along the Volga and its tributaries. Typical sites show remains of settlements, walled and placed in defensible positions, often on steep or overhanging banks of rivers. The people were farmers and stockbreeders living in wooden dwellings, and their most important animal was the horse. Many pins, needles, arrowheads, and harpoons of bone were discovered, and some simple hand-made pottery showing the marks of woven fabrics. Metal objects were usually of bronze, but occasionally of iron.

In the west such strongholds as that of Dyakovo near Moscow show little trace of contact with mounted nomads, but in the east in the basin of the Kama the walled towns and burial grounds named after Ananyino near Elabuga have yielded remains of a mixed culture which might be called Finno-Scythic, lasting from 600 to 400 B C. Animals are very commonly represented in small bronzes modelled on those of the Scythian Animal style later to be described; they are often heavily furred animals

23, 24 The curled beast represented on this bronze ornament from Ananyino is closely modelled on the Scythian style of curled beasts found all over the steppes. Equally Finno-Scythic is the figure on a tombstone from Ananyino (*Ill. 24*) wearing trousers, tunic, belt and peculiar conical hat. The large torque round the neck is also distinctive

whose skins could have been exported southward. A human figure incised on a tombstone wears something like Scythian costume; a tunic, trousers, conical hat, torque, belt, dagger and gorytus.

Men's bodies have been found buried with swords and daggers, and women's with bags, mirrors, beads and metal ornaments.

Remains of the Ananyino culture show Caucasian and Siberian influences, as well as Scythian features, and Greek objects which must have come from the Pontic coast. Herodotus describes a Scythian trade-route which led in this direction and was used also by Greeks.

The Cimmerians (c. 800 BC)

The mounted nomads created a peculiar form of society which outlasted the ancient civilizations of the Near East and of the classical world. It was perfectly adapted to the steppes, especially where they would not support agriculture; where agriculture was possible and the cultivators were tenacious, the nomads levied tribute from them, as in South Russia. It was a tribal society, in which particular tribes of nomads became for a time Royal Hordes and ruled other nomads in feudal fashion. One Royal Horde could easily be overthrown, and then with

25 This sword-hilt from Ananyino is of the Scythian type with ears modelled on Central European types

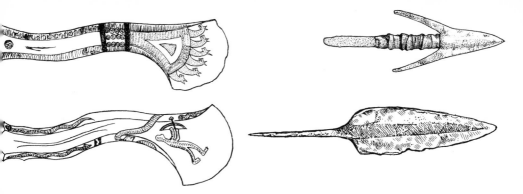

26, 27 Bronze battle-axes (*Ill. 26*) of the Koban culture by their curved form and the ornamentation engraved on the blade are clearly distinguished from the straight Scythian axe-heads (*cf. Ill. 29*). The earlier bronze arrowheads (*Ill. 27*) of Transcaucasia and Luristan are flat and tanged, quite different from the trilobate Scythian examples (*cf. Ill. 33*). *c.* 1000–800 BC

all its subjects become itself subject to a new Royal Horde. The later history of the steppes consists of a repetition of this change on varying scales, and of collisions between the nomads and civilized peoples. Hunting peoples from the forests were also recruited to nomadism by direct example. All the peoples were in continual movement over their ranges of pasture, but did not migrate unless they were driven.

On the South Russian Steppes the first approximation to a mounted nomad power was that of people known in classical sources as the Cimmerians, who ruled north of the Caucasus and on the Pontic Steppes, with an extension into Hungary. From the names of the chiefs, preserved in Assyrian accounts of their attacks on Near Eastern peoples, it is now commonly taken that the rulers were Iranians, though their subjects were probably of other groups also, for instance Thracians and Caucasians. The origin of the Cimmerians is hard to trace. They may have originated in the North Caucasian culture, advancing northwards to conquer the Pontic Steppes and part of the Danubian plain where new types of harness equipment of Koban style appear *c.* 800 BC.

The stylistic link between Koban and Luristanian metal-work suggests that the Cimmerians penetrated into

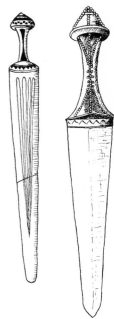

28 Pre-Scythian swords and daggers from Transcaucasia are of Near Eastern type and have not the eared hilts of some Scythian swords as in *Ill. 34*

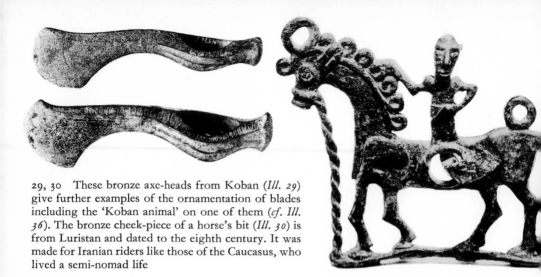

29, 30   These bronze axe-heads from Koban (*Ill. 29*) give further examples of the ornamentation of blades including the 'Koban animal' on one of them (*cf. Ill. 36*). The bronze cheek-piece of a horse's bit (*Ill. 30*) is from Luristan and dated to the eighth century. It was made for Iranian riders like those of the Caucasus, who lived a semi-nomad life

Iran, while grave finds on the Dniepr and Don have also been attributed to them. Finally the Don basin catacomb-graves have been taken as Cimmerian, the succeeding timber-graves being early Scythian, *c.* 900 BC, or later.

In general history the Cimmerians are chiefly famous for their invasion of Asia Minor in 680–670 BC which, according to Herodotus, was the result of their flight from the Scythians. They left the Pontic Steppes and crossed the Caucasus, leaving a small remnant behind fortifications in the Taman Peninsula, east of the straits of Kerch, the ancient Cimmerian Bosporus. In spite of Herodotus, the movement of peoples may have begun earlier than the Scythian invasion of their country. But at any rate he must be correct in saying that they crossed the mountains farther west than the Scythians, who went by the Caspian coast to Media. An alternative route would lead them into Armenia, and it is there that they appear late in the eighth century on the northern border of the kingdom of Urartu as the Gimirrai or Gamir of Assyrian records. The crown prince Sennacherib reports to his father Sargon (721–705 BC), at war with Urartu, that its king Rusas has been heavily defeated by the Cimmerians.

Ill. 31

The Cimmerians, while occupying northern Urartu, appear finally as allies of the Urartians against Assyria

52

31 The black-figure scenes on the lid of this terracotta sarcophagus from Klazomenai on the coast of Asia Minor dated to sixth or early fifth century BC include mounted warriors, who may be Cimmerian invaders of *c.* 680–670 BC. So possibly may the charioteers. Both are enemies of the panoplied Greeks, and are accompanied by wolf-like dogs. The artist himself lived later under the Persian peace

and then advance westward. In 695 BC they destroyed the kingdom of Phrygia and afterwards dominated central Anatolia in the time of Sennacherib (704–681 BC). They overran Lydia, devastated the Greek cities of the coast, such as Ephesus, Magnesia and Smyrna, and finally turned south against Cilicia, then an Assyrian province. The remnant of the Cimmerians in Anatolia eventually settled west of Armenia in Cappadocia. Others, who had passed along the eastern border of Assyria, reached the Zagros mountains where they may have been absorbed by the Medes.

In the Scythian period the Siberian and Central Asian Steppes were occupied by Sarmatian peoples akin to the Scythians. All these peoples were mounted nomads, and their decorative art included some version of the Animal Style described below. All wore the tunic, trousers, boots and cap, and carried the bowcases, bows, arrows, swords and axes represented as theirs in Greek and Persian art. In metallurgy some had adopted iron besides bronze, while others still used bronze only. For transport they had elaborate waggons, in South Russia sometimes with two or even three compartments.

32 Pottery models of covered wagons used on the steppes; right, two-wheeled *c.* 2000 BC; above, four-wheeled *c.* 600 BC

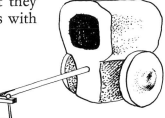

CHAPTER FOUR

The Scythians

In South Russia the Scythians occupied the former Cimmerian territory, except the Taman Peninsula and part of the Crimea, and for a time they did not cross the Dniestr to Bessarabia and the Danube valley and farther, where later remains of theirs are found. Archaeologically the earliest Scythians are a problem, because they did not develop their distinctive art style until the sixth century, as dated by Greek objects found with its oldest specimens, and the style has no ancestry in South Russia. If we identify the catacomb tombs as Cimmerian, we can regard the timber-graves that follow them as early Scythian. These, like the catacomb-graves, extend into Caucasia and even round the eastern end of the range through Daghestan. In Transcaucasia they would represent Scythians of an earlier immigration direct from the Volga Steppe, who perhaps drove on the Median and Persian tribes into Iran.

The main Scythian migration under the Royal Horde, the only one known to Herodotus, flowed first into South Russia. Then, drawn perhaps by their kinsmen's stories of rich plunder, the Scythians passed the mountains to invade Western Asia. The main body arrived in the Mannaean country around Lake Urmia, but some at least must have destroyed the Urartian town of Teishe-

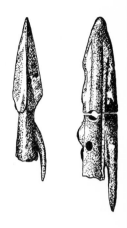

33 Bronze arrowheads of the seventh to sixth century BC socketed to receive the shaft. They are trilobate (in section like a three-cornered star), a shape which gave greater strength, and have a long barb

bani (modern Karmir Blur in Soviet Armenia), where their distinctive trilobate arrowheads were found sticking in the walls. The remains show that other Scythians were among the defenders. The Scythians remained in Western Asia for a generation or two during the last days of Assyria. The two nations became allies, and remained allied until the last. After the time of Asarhaddon and Assurbanipal the Scythians plundered some of the provinces of the weakened Assyrian Empire, but were still, if Herodotus is right, so far its allies and guests that Cyaxares the Mede had to break their power before he could destroy Nineveh in 612 BC. After their defeat by the Medes, they returned through the Caucasus to the Pontic Steppes, leaving some of their number behind in the Armenian districts of Scythene and Sacasene, and elsewhere. They had given Western Asia its first taste of domination by mounted nomads, and are remembered in Hebrew prophecy and later apocalyptic writings as the hosts of Gog and Magog.

The Animal Style

We now come to one of the most exciting manifestations of the nomad peoples of the steppes – their creation of an individual and vigorous art style which still has power to intrigue and fascinate. It is an art of pattern and ornament, using some techniques which may have originated in carving wood, bone and horn, and others of later origin which belong to metal-work only, by which it is chiefly represented. It was also practised in wood, leather-work and textiles. Naturalistic motifs, especially those based on animals, are subordinated to a strong sense of rhythm and design, and built up into fantastic

34 Scythian bronze swords of the same date as the arrowheads above have eared hilts recalling those of the Early Iron Age in Central Europe

55

arrangements of compelling aesthetic quality. It is the antithesis of the naturalistic art of the village and urban communities of the settled agriculturalists: human representations scarcely exist, portraiture never, and literal transcripts of nature are shunned. Just as the pattern of life of the nomad contrasts at every point with that of the farmer or townsman, so too the pattern of the art produced on the steppes has its individual and arresting qualities. Made by people on the move, it is lavished on portable objects such as decorations on weapons or the equipment for horse and rider; the outcome of a heroic society, it is an art of display and ostentation. Precious metals, especially gold, are used in profusion: it is essentially an aristocratic art, like that of the Celts.

Our knowledge of Scythian art is almost wholly gained by the excavation of the royal or semi-royal tombs of their nobility and aristocracy, where, as we shall see, the dead were buried with barbaric pomp. These tombs began to be made by the Scythians in the Kuban basin, and later on the Dniepr, only after their return from Western Asia. There are several strands of tradition which combine to make Scythian art what it is, a unique creation resulting in something new, rich and strange.

A northern strand from the wooded steppe has often been suggested as the original. This may be shared with the Karasuk animal style already mentioned. But there were obviously other strands of equal importance. *Ill. 35* One strand came from Anatolia; for instance the antlered stag, a favourite Scythian theme, appears already with head and neck treated somewhat in the Scythian fashion on stone reliefs from Alaca Hüyük in Anatolia of about the fourteenth century BC, and even earlier from the Royal Tombs there as a metal figure to be fastened on a pole-top in the Scythian manner. From the Transcaucasian Bronze Age various sites of the native Gandsha–Karabagh culture, such as Kayakent, have produced bronze belt-plates

35 This figure of a stag in copper and electrum from Alaca Hüyük in northern Anatolia is older than 2000 BC but is ancestral to the much later Scythian stag-figures

36 A bronze belt-plate from Kiev (below) seems to combine Caucasian and Scythian features. It has not yet the classic Scythian style but an earlier more geometric manner; it should be earlier than the seventh century BC. A belt-plate from Kayakent, Transcaucasia (left), is purely Caucasian work. Contrast the animals with the Koban animal shown right

bearing animal figures that seem to show a development from formal geometric shape and arrangement to livelier and freer forms more akin to the Scythian. A bronze belt found near Kiev combines Transcaucasian animal forms with something like animal combat between a stag and a beast of prey and a heraldic opposition of beasts. Another animal style is that of the Lelvar culture of the Trans-caucasian Iron Age, but this is different, and has human figures of bowmen as the reliefs of Alaca Hüyük have, and even chariots. The Koban culture has fantastic animal figures, used particularly to decorate bronze belt-plates and axe-blades, but it also has representations of bowmen,

Ill. 36

Ill. 39

Ill. 26

37–39 A lioness and cub, showing some approach to the Scythian style, decorate this bronze axe-head from Lake Van (*Ill. 37*), made in the Luristanian style of 900 BC or later. The manner is still relatively smooth and naturalistic. The axe-head is less obviously a ceremonial piece than many of its kind. Objects of the style are not confined to Luristan. More typical of Luristan is the digitated bronze axe-head (*Ill. 38*) with its edge set at an unpractical angle and the digitations beyond the haft-pole ending in animal heads. The carved slab of the thirteenth century from Alaca Hüyük (*Ill. 39*, below) shows affinities with Caucasian art. The stag shown is a forerunner of Scythian art, the boar and hunter above it have later affinities in Transcaucasia and Luristan

Ills. 37, 38, 43 and it delights in small bronze figures of riders. Farther south the bronzes of Luristan have representations of animals and even animal-combats, executed in a style which seems to anticipate the Scythian, but they also have human figures as a prominent feature.

40–42 The gold band inlaid with animal figures in blue paste (*Ill. 40*, above) is from the treasure of Ziwiye. The shape and pose of the crouching animal and its alternating direction are Scythian. An inlaid silver dish, of which a detail is shown here (*Ill. 41*, right) is another object from Ziwiye. It is about 14 inches across and is inlaid with ten rings of golden figures of animals between the boss and the outer ring, both of an Iranian petal ornament. The lynxes, running hares and bird heads are Scythian. The general arrangement is perhaps Urartian. Hieroglyphic signs, perhaps of Urartian origin, seem to give directions for assembling the separately made pieces. An outlying example of Scythian art, now dated fairly late in the Scythian period, is the celebrated fish-shaped shield-ornament (*Ill. 42*, below) found at Vettersfelde, now in East Germany. It is of pale gold, executed in repoussé and covered with animals in relief which include other fish, a sort of bearded sea-sphinx, a falcon, a leopard attacking a boar and a lion attacking a deer. The tail-fins are converted into rams' heads in Scythian fashion

43–48 This ceremonial axe from Uzbekistan, Central Asia, dated *c.* 1000–800 BC is of bronze inlaid with silver. It shows a tiger which has brought down a wild goat and is itself attacked. The traditional Scythian stag (*Ill. 44*, below) appears at Kul Oba, Crimea, in the fifth century, in a less lively version than earlier figures and ornamented with figures of other animals, somewhat spoiled by Greek influence. The gold scabbard (*Ill. 45*, opposite above) from Litoi on the Lower Dniepr shows Median influence, if not origin. The celebrated gold pectoral ornament from Ziwiye (*Ill. 46*) is now usually dated to the seventh century BC. It has been suggested that it belonged to the Scythian chief Bartatua, who allied himself with the Assyrians. The gold eagle-griffin's head from Ziwiye (*Ill. 47*) is Urartian. Another sheet of gold from the Ziwiye treasure (*Ill. 48*) shows a pattern of alternating stags and ibexes. The stags with drawn-up legs and laid-back horns are exactly in the Scythian style of South Russia

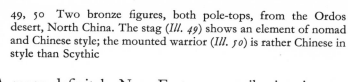

49, 50 Two bronze figures, both pole-tops, from the Ordos desert, North China. The stag (*Ill. 49*) shows an element of nomad and Chinese style; the mounted warrior (*Ill. 50*) is rather Chinese in style than Scythic

A more definitely Near Eastern contribution is suggested by the figures on gold plate found in the treasure of Ziwiye in Kurdistan, the ancient Mannaean country. There the artist has combined animal figures recognizable as Scythian with features of Assyrian, Mannaean and Urartian art, so that it has been suggested that the treasure belonged to Bartatua, the Scythian king allied to the Assyrians around 670 BC. This is certainly the nearest approach to the early Scythian style of the Kuban.

Something like the Scythian Animal Style was adopted by all the mounted nomads as far as the borders of China by the end of the first millennium BC. The various traditions of this art continued to be influenced by Iranian art of the Median and Achaemenid periods from the sixth to the fourth centuries BC.

The Scythian style proper, as we shall see, is very closely reproduced at a great distance and during the same period in the nomad chiefs' tombs of the Altai, belonging to the Maiemir and Pazyryk periods. In a less striking degree it appears again in the Tagar culture of the Minusinsk basin, where more or less settled metal-working tribes lived under nomad domination, much in the fashion of the Ananyino tribes of the Kama. Later varieties of the Animal Style, which may loosely be called Sarmatian, are found over a great area between China and Europe, but particularly in southern and western Siberia. The Sarmatian tradition, like the Scythian before it, is also reflected in the well-known small bronzes from the Gobi and from the Ordos desert of North China and neighbouring regions.

Ills. 49, 50,
108–110

The favourite animals of the Scythian style are the stag, the horse, the ibex, the boar, the bear, the wolf, feline beasts of prey not always identifiable, the eagle, often represented by its head alone, and, in some remarkable

51–54 The Scythians of Hungary are represented by this electrum plaque of a stag, perhaps of the fifth century, from Tapioszentmarton. Though it is in the classic pose and not cluttered with ornament, its shape is less clear and its pose clumsy and limp as compared with such earlier examples as the stag of Kostromskaya (*Ill. 71*). The pole-top (*Ill. 52*) representing a stag dates from the late Chou period of China whilst an elk (*Ill. 53*) surmounts a later example of the Han period. Both are typically Chinese. Another bronze pole-top (*Ill. 54*) from Ulski Aul in the Kuban (seventh to sixth century BC) has its shape suggested by an eagle's head; it bears a tiny ibex in relief

examples, fish of uncertain species. These animals are all wild, except perhaps the horse; they were mostly feared as enemies or hunted as game, and most belong to the forests and mountains rather than to the open steppe. They are much more dramatic subjects than the tame animals on which nomadism depends. Still more so are the mythical monsters such as lion-griffins and eagle-griffins. The stag in a variety of conventional poses is more common than any other animal. It is worth noting that the name Saka, commonest of all names applied to the Iranian nomads by themselves and by others, actually means 'stag'.

The animal figures no doubt had a religious significance for peoples who believed in animal ancestors or in spirits in animal form which could help the soul to reach the next world. They were also perhaps badges of the tribes or clans of mounted warriors who formed an aristocracy on the steppes.

55, 56 Two gold plates from wooden rhytons from the Seven Brothers Barrow in the Kuban show a winged panther attacking a goat (left) and an eagle killing a hare (right). The second is a well-known theme in Greek art and the style of both plates is Graeco-Scythian

57 On the back of the famous silver and gilt mirror from Kelermes are figures of a mixed Graeco-Oriental, or Graeco-Scythian style. The figure shown is probably the Great Mother in her Anatolian form of Cybele, holding her lions in the classic beast-taming posture of the Near East

Scythian Religion

Among the Scythians, as among the ancient peoples, art was closely connected with religion. Some authorities think that the scenes of animal combat may have represented conflicts between the divine powers that controlled the world. It is known that the northern nomads had a strong element of Shamanism in their religion: that they used professional visionaries and medicine-men who were expert in dealing with the world of spirits and gave advice to kings and chiefs. These are mentioned in Herodotus, who also gives some indication of the Scythian pantheon as it appeared to Greeks, comparing Tabiti to Hestia, Papaeus to Zeus, Api to Earth, Goetosyrus to Apollo, Argimpasa to Aphrodite Urania, Thagimasadas to Posidon. There was also a war-god, whose native name is not given, but who was often represented in the form of a sacred sword as later among the Sarmatians and the Huns.

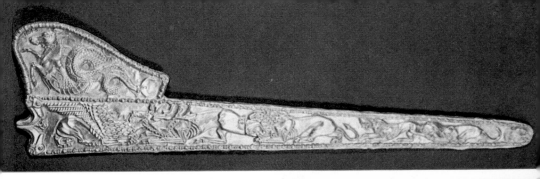

58–61 The gold scabbard from Kul Oba (*Ill. 58*, above), perhaps of the fourth century, has a row of animal figures which are pervaded by Greek influence. A file of crouching lions appears with its first member biting into the haunch of a deer, which is also attacked from the front by an eagle-griffin. On the attachment is a sea-serpent with the forequarters and head of a horse. The famous electrum vase from Kul Oba (*Ills. 59–61*) is purely Greek work devoted to typical Scythian scenes. Its date lies in the fourth century when Scythians and Greeks had been long acquainted. The first scene (right) shows a man treating his companion for a mouth-wound; the second (below, left) the binding of a leg-wound; in the third (below, right) a Scythian bow is strung. The clothes and gear are admirably shown, and also the physical type, which is entirely European. The crouching, kneeling and squatting postures are no doubt real, though they are also required by the space

62 The outer surface of an elaborately chased gold phiale shows a repetitive pattern of Greek Gorgon-heads alternating with smaller mens' heads which have drooping moustaches and must be Scythian. Minute boars' heads are inserted round the belly of the vessel, while dolphins occupy a circular frieze near its centre. The technique is Greek, except perhaps for the extreme crowding of formal ornamentation between the figures

Ill. 57

Scythian art, which is not confined to the Animal Style, also has representations of the Great Goddess who controlled the fertility of pastures and animals. She appears most notably on a silver-and-gilt mirror from Kelermes, which owes much to Near Eastern art, on fragments of a rhyton from Merdjany, and a gold plaque belonging to a tiara from Karagodeuashkh, all of them sites in the Kuban.

Thus Scythian religion combined northern and Near Eastern elements. Its massive emphasis on the world of spirits, where the ghosts of the newly dead chiefs needed to be well-equipped and attended, appears in all that is known of tombs and funeral rites.

The Royal Tombs

The tombs of the Scythian kings and chiefs have long been famous in archaeology. In construction they have much in common with the far older barrows of the Kuban

63–66 A number of gold plaques and
ornaments, probably used as decoration on
clothing, were found at Kul Oba. Nearly all
show a large amount of Greek influence in
their style and subject. These three square
gold plaques show respectively two women
dancing in long Scythian dress (*Ill. 63*); the
winged horse Pegasus of Greek myth (*Ill. 64*),
and a Scythian horseman pursuing a hare
with a javelin (*Ill. 65*). This feat, mentioned
by Herodotus, gave practice in hitting a
moving target. On another plaque from Kul
Oba (*Ill. 66*) two Scythians are represented
drinking out of the same horn in a ceremony
of blood-brotherhood, such as is known
among many nomad peoples. Herodotus
says that the Scythians when they made a
treaty poured wine into a great clay bowl,
drew blood from themselves and mingled it
with the wine, dipped a sword, arrows, a
battle-axe and a javelin into it, cursed future
traitors, and finally drank together

67, 68   The gold bracelet (left) has terminals in the form of sphinx's heads of Greek style and that on the right has terminals in the form of lion's heads of Greek type. Both are from Kul Oba and were found on a male and a female body respectively

already described, while in contents they show an analogous mixture of northern and Near Eastern objects and styles. This continuity in idea cannot be traced on the steppes, and should probably be sought in Western Asia, which now provides a new impulse.

The most notable groups of tombs are in the Kuban basin, often in the same places as the first great barrows (see map, p. 35), in the Taman Peninsula, in the Crimea, and on the Dniepr where they extend to the neighbourhood of Kiev. Other burials occur in the Danubian plain, and outlying single graves even in North Germany; there are more on the Don and Donetz and farther east by the Volga to the Urals. From the Kuban westward, as time passes, the contents show increasing Greek influence.

Ills. 44, 58–70 This Greek influence is particularly strong in the remains from Kul Oba, one of those tombs of the fourth century BC near Kerch in the Crimea, which have burial

69, 70   In the scenes portrayed on this silver and parcel-gilt vase from Kul Oba, a griffin attacks a goat, a lion and lioness a stag, and a lion a boar. The manner is again Greek; the themes are alike Greek and oriental

chambers vaulted with Greek stonework. With the king's skeleton and those of a male and a female attendant were a gold-plated scabbard, three vases, one of silver, one of silver-gilt and one of electrum, and many smaller objects of gold, all of them Greek work but adorned with figures to suit Scythian taste. Some pieces of ivory veneer from the inside of the king's coffin were covered with beautiful Greek drawings of scenes from Greek myth. Objects of Scythian origin were few and of less interest.

The Account of Herodotus

A celebrated description of the tombs and the funeral rites is given by Herodotus, who is to a great extent confirmed by excavation. This is as follows: 'The tombs of the kings are in the land of the Gerrhi. There, when their king dies, they dig a great square pit. When they have prepared this they take up the corpse, its body smeared over with wax and its belly slit open, cleaned out, and filled with chopped frankincense, parsley and anise, and then sewn up again and bring it on a waggon to another tribe. These who receive the corpse when it is brought do as the Royal Scythians. They cut a piece out of their ears, cut their hair short, slash their arms, slit their foreheads and noses, and thrust arrows through their left hands. Then they convey the corpse to another tribe among their subjects, and the tribe first reached goes with them. When they have gone round all the tribes with the corpse, they are among the Gerrhi, who live farthest off of all their subjects, and among the tombs.

'When they have laid the corpse upon a mattress in its chamber, they stick spears into the ground on all sides. Then they lay beams across and cover these with wicker, and in the remaining space of the tomb they strangle and bury one concubine, the cupbearer, a cook, a groom, an attendant and a messenger; they also bury the pick of everything else and golden vessels. They use no silver or bronze. When they have done this, they heap up a great mound, vying with one another and full of eagerness to make it as great as they can. Then when a year has passed they do as follows. They take the most suitable of the other attendants – these are true-born Scythians and are called to attend him by the king himself, for they have no bought slaves – and strangle fifty of them and fifty of the finest horses. They take out their entrails, clean them, fill them with chaff and sew them up. Then they put half the rim of a wheel with the hollow side upwards on two stakes, and the other half-rim on two others, fixing many such frames, drive stout stakes lengthwise through the horses to their necks and hoist them on to the rims. The front rims support the horses' shoulders and the rear ones their thighs and bellies, while both pairs of legs hang free. They put reins and bridles on the horses, draw these forward and tie them to pegs. They then hoist every one

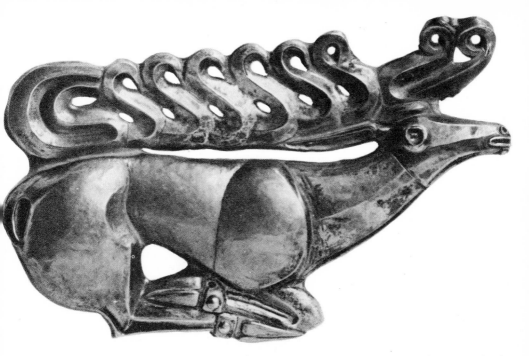

71 This typically Scythian stag represented on a gold plaque from the barrow of Kostromskaya in the Kuban recalls the stag figures of Ziwiye in *Ill. 48*. Seventh to sixth century BC

of the strangled youths on to his horse, after driving a vertical stake through him by the spine to the neck, and part of this stake that projects downward they fasten into a socket in the other stake that runs through the horse. When they have set up riders in this style round the tomb they ride off.'

Herodotus also says that after a funeral the Scythians used to purify themselves by inhaling the fumes of hemp from seeds scattered on red-hot stones inside tents of felt. As they did this they howled in delight at the vapour-bath. This custom he hardly understands.

Ill. 90

This account can be compared with the results of excavation. The circles of impaled horses and riders, if they existed, would soon be destroyed by beasts and birds and the weather. But later nomad peoples in Siberia have had the custom of impaling horses for sacrifice until very

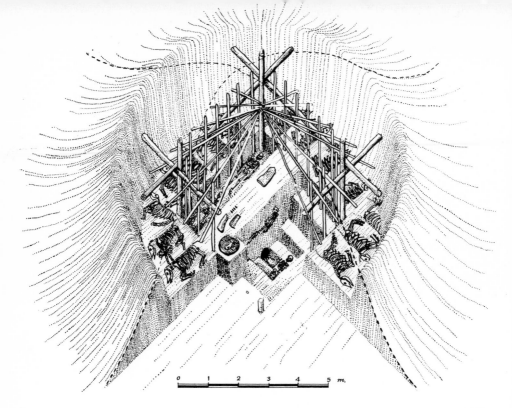

72 The barrow of Kostromskaya reconstructed in the present sketch is an example of the older and simpler type of Scythian royal tomb from which later types were elaborated. The wooden framework, the human skeleton and the skeletons of sacrificed horses are shown as described in the text. This barrow and others of the Kuban and Lower Dniepr should represent the stage immediately following the Royal Scythians' return through the Caucasus from Western Asia, perhaps with captive craftsmen

recent times. The tombs themselves confirm Herodotus in many details. The profusion of finds is such that one or two burials, briefly described, must stand for all.

Scythian Burials in the Kuban

In the Kuban region an earlier stage is represented by such burials as those of Kostromskaya and Kelermes. At Kostromskaya the burial chamber was marked out by four great posts. Beams were laid crosswise about them to form a square of side 10 feet 6 inches and held in place by rows of much smaller and shorter posts. Roof beams were added between the posts sloping upward to form

Ill. 72

73, 74 The golden plaque of a panther from Kelermes with cloisonné inlay in ears and paws is entirely oriental. It was probably attached to the breast-piece of a scaled corselet. A unique find is the gold-mounted iron axe from Kelermes (*Ill. 74*) which is adorned with figures of stags and other animals in the style known from Ziwiye, and also with two animal-headed figures facing inward to an Urartian spear-symbol. The oriental affinities of the axe and the panther are as marked as the Greek affinities of the mirror (*Ill. 57*)

the frame of a pyramidal roof. In the square about 7 feet below ground were the dead man's belongings: an iron scale hauberk with copper scales on the shoulders and lower edge, four iron spearheads, a thin round shield of iron adorned in the centre with a cast gold plaque of a stag, two leather quivers, some bronze arrowheads, several copper and iron bits, and a large whetstone and pottery, all deliberately broken. The square space had been filled with earth, rolled hard, which contained thirteen skeletons but nothing with them. At the very bottom was a small chamber closed with two slabs of stone, but this was empty. The wooden structure had

Ill. 71

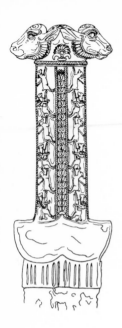

75 On the gold hilt of the great sword from Chertomlyk on the Dniepr are running processions in relief of alternate chamois and mounted hunters, and outward facing ox-heads on the top

apparently been set alight before the earth was heaped on it. Outside the square were the skeletons of twenty-two horses buried in pairs, some with bits in their mouths.

In one barrow at Kelermes the chief's body was untouched. He wore a bronze helmet, surrounded by two broad gold diadems, one with rosettes, flowers and falcons of gold soldered to it, the other with flowers only. A short dagger by his right hand had a gold haft, and a gold sheath with a row of monsters and genii, and on its side projection a crouching stag. An iron axe was decorated on haft and head with genii and beasts in gold. To the left was a golden panther surrounded by iron scales: its eyes and nostrils were filled by glass pastes with stones inset, and its ears decorated with glass pastes set in cloisons of gold. The dagger and panther are in the Mesopotamian style of the eighth and seventh centuries BC.

The Chertomlyk Burial

Of the royal tombs on the Dniepr, the great burial of Chertomlyk may be taken as an example. The mound was 60 feet high and 1,100 feet round, and the main chamber measured 15 feet 7 inches at the top, widening downwards to a depth of 35 feet 6 inches. Four side-chambers opened out from this, one from each corner, and the fourth of these again into a fifth. In the main chamber, which had been very much plundered, were traces of a coffin or bier painted red and bright blue. In the south-east chamber were a cauldron, remains of a skeleton, knives, arrows, traces of a carpet, gold plates and strips which had been sewn to clothes, and iron hooks in the walls and ceilings for hanging clothes. In the north-east chamber were six amphorae, a bronze mirror, a skeleton with a bronze torque, earrings and finger-rings of gold, remains of a whip-handle of ivory and gold, 399 gold strips representing animals, monsters, and in a few cases scenes from Greek myth, and many more gold ornaments.

Ill. 78

76, 77 The silver and gilt vase from Chertomlyk is entirely Greek work, but probably held Scythian *koumiss*. This would have been poured in through the neck, which has a strainer, and would have flowed out when the animal-headed spouts, also with strainers, were unplugged. A band near the neck is occupied with griffins seizing prey; a lower one with Scythians breaking in and harnessing two breeds of horses. The plants and birds of the decoration are hardly Scythian

In the south-west chamber lay a skeleton with a golden torque bearing twelve figures of lions, remains of a hood and twenty-five gold plates, in the form of griffins, bracelets, a brass-plated belt, greaves, vessels of gold and bronze, a quiver with arrows, and a whip. Beside this was another skeleton with similar equipment. In the north-west chamber, on remains of a bier painted dark and light blue, lay a woman's skeleton with earrings and gold plates by the head, and covered there and on the upper body with a purple veil bearing fifty-seven gold plates outlining the shape of a hood. By this lay a man's skeleton with bracelets and knives. In the west of the chamber was the famous Chertomlyk vase, made of silver and engraved with plants and birds, and also with a frieze representing Scythians breaking in horses, surmounted with another frieze of griffins. By it was a great

Ills. 76, 77

78 A purely Greek plaque showing Herakles strangling the Nemean lion, from Chertomlyk

Ills. 79, 80

silver dish engraved with acanthus leaves and the figure of a woman. The last two are Greek work. In the fifth chamber were cauldrons and a heap of gold, and plunder from the king's body, including the great gold plates from his bowcase and sword-sheath engraved with Greek scenes and griffins. Outside this group were three graves of horses bridled with gold and silver and two of grooms with silver or gold torques and quivers of arrows.

We can now imagine the funeral procession, led by standard-bearers with beast emblems mounted on poles and others waving bronze rattles on poles and shrieking. The king's body would follow on a waggon, probably under a canopy supported by poles with beast emblems, adorned with gold plaques of beasts and monsters, and hung with bells. The concubines, the servants and the grooms with saddled and bridled horses would come next, and finally the great crowd of cropped and gashed mourners wailing and howling. At the tomb the women, servants and grooms would be strangled and the horses killed with a blow from an axe on the head. The royal body in its festal robe would be laid on its bier in the centre of the chamber, at full length with its head to the east, and weapons and vessels full of food placed ready to hand. The walls would be hung with brightly dyed

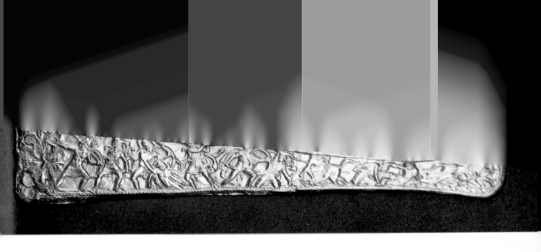

79, 80   This gold-plated scabbard from Chertomlyk (above) is Greek work of the second quality, not well composed. The griffin attacking a stag on the attachment is a Scythian subject. The human figures are Greeks and Persians in battle. Some of the Persians are mounted. Most of the Greeks are unrealistically nude apart from shields and weapons. The gold plate from the bowcase, or *gorytus*, of Chertomlyk (below) is entirely Greek in the style of its decorative figures, only its shape and purpose being Scythian. The human scenes represent Achilles on Scyros among the daughters of Lycomedes, who kept him as a girl to save him from warfare, until Odysseus arrived, disguised as a trader, and produced a sword among his wares. The composition is not good. The design may be one of many copies

and embroidered felt and the floor covered with carpets to reproduce the sumptuous interior of the royal tent. The grooms and horses nearby in their places of burial would be ready to accompany their master with due pomp on his journey through the afterworld.

The Scythians and the Greek Settlements on the Russian Coast

Before we leave the Scythians some mention must be made of the Greek colonies on the South Russian coast where Herodotus collected so much information. The most important cities were Tyras on the Dniestr, Olbia on the Bug, Chersonnesus and Theodosia on the Crimean coast, Pantikapaion on the same coast facing east across the straits of Kerch, Tanais at the mouth of the Don, and Phanagoria on the Taman Peninsula. They and smaller settlements were tolerated by the Scythians and other natives for the sake of the wine and oil and Greek manufactures, which they exchanged against Scythian corn, hides, furs, timber and slaves. But there was not much mixture of race or culture. In the third century a Scythian capital was founded and fortified at Neapolis in the Crimea, when the Scythians had lost most of the steppe to the Sarmatians. The Greek sites and Scythian Neapolis have long been excavated by Russian archaeologists.

The Pazyryk Burials

The funeral customs of the Pontic Scythians have now been further illustrated by discoveries in a region remote from the Greeks, the High Altai. There in the famous tombs of Pazyryk nomads related to the Scythians buried their chiefs under stone-topped barrows, which preserved normally perishable things, including human bodies. The stone has had the effect of freezing the contents in ice, very little altered for more than twenty-

Ills. 81–83

Ill. 95

81, 82 Greek work again is the gold comb from Solokha near the Lower Dniepr, adorned with a group of two foot-soldiers in Scythian dress, with breastplates, lunate shields and short swords, one without a helmet, in combat with a rider in the same dress and armour except for a Greek helmet and a spear. If the figures really represent natives, the fighters are perhaps Scythians of different tribes. Greeks would hardly dress so

three centuries, particularly where more water was let in through robbers' shafts. The chambers are of the usual square timber-lined kind, and the contents are closely like those of the South Russian tombs, though much less rich in metal. The influence of Western Asia of the Persian period is strongly present, and in the place of added Greek influence there is here Chinese.

Ill. 96

The horses buried round the chambers were in many cases not the small Mongolian breed of the steppes, but tall thoroughbred animals such as were famous in Bactria and Media, and their stomachs contained the remains of grain, not of the expected grass, showing they had been carefully stabled and fed. In some cases they wore masks of leather and felt, representing reindeer or griffins, which were evidently of magical importance.

Ill. 88

79

83 Another remarkable example of Greek work for the Scythian market is a gold brooch, perhaps from Pantikapaion (Kerch), dated to the fifth century B C; a very sumptuous ornament, though the griffin and horse-headed sea-serpent are not the liveliest of their kind. Brooches in the nomad world are more likely to belong to women's dress

84–86 The features of a Scythian queen, probably of the third century A D, are represented in this exceptional gold mask found on her skull at Glinishche, near Kerch, in an area which was long a refuge for Scythians from the steppes. She was buried in a marble sarcophagus and wrapped in a woollen robe embroidered and adorned with gold. Many articles found with her were much older heirlooms. The cap (*Ill. 85*, below) from Cape Ak-burun, Crimea, was lined with leather and made of pieces of goldwork in plant design. An amphora and a coin in the grave suggests a Greek owner. The riders on the lid of the bronze *lebes* (*Ill. 86*, opposite) from Campania are probably Scythians. Two of them are delivering the backward 'Parthian shot' characteristic of the nomads. Unusual features are the helmet in the shape of a swan's head worn by two riders, and the shorts(?), worn by all

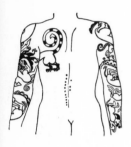

87 The upper part of the chieftain's body from the second tomb at Pazyryk was tattooed in patterns of nomad animal style. This was perhaps general in men

The most remarkable tomb was the second. The floor and walls had been largely covered with black felt secured with pegs and bronze nails. The furniture included low wooden tables that could be taken to pieces, wooden food-vessels, a drum shaped like an hour-glass and ornamented with gold leaf, and a stringed instrument like a lute. A double coffin 4·20 metres long lay empty, covered with birch bark and leather appliqué, and lined with black felt and carpet; it would have taken two bodies on end. Among articles of clothing were a long woman's coat of squirrel fur, hairs outward, edged with horse-hide, and a matching stomacher edged with sable and other fur; a long, wide man's shirt of plant fibres, and two pairs of women's fur boots, one of leopard skin and ornamented on soft soles with a pattern of crystals, so that they may have been worn in cross-legged position to show the soles turned upward.

On top of an original layer of clear ice, and held in a mass of dirty yellow ice from the later inflow, lay the bodies of the chief and his wife, torn from their coffin. The woman was about forty years old, tall and graceful and of European type. Her hair had been shaved off and her head trepanned to remove the brain, which had been replaced with plant material, after which the scalp was sewn up again; her entrails had been removed through a long slit in the belly and similarly replaced with plant material before the skin was sewn up again. A long plait of her hair, soft, black, and wavy, lay near by in a case of its own. The man was about sixty, of mongoloid type and powerfully built. He had been killed in battle by two axe-strokes through his skull, and had been scalped before his own men recovered him and fitted him out with a false scalp sewn on. He too had been embalmed, and in early life had been tattooed with designs in the

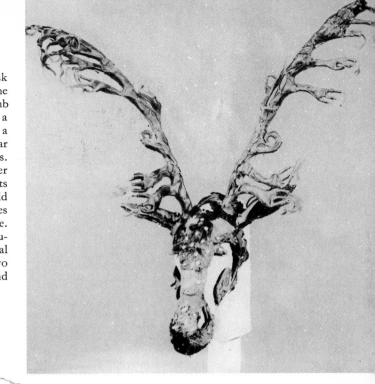

88, 89 A reindeer-mask from the head of one of the best horses in the first tomb at Pazyryk probably had a magical significance like a griffin-mask and similar masks from other tombs. Possibly ghostly reindeer were the appropriate mounts for reaching the other world and the sacrificed horses would need such a disguise. The wooden stringed instrument (below) is a conjectural reconstruction based on two examples found in the second tomb at Pazyryk

best Animal Style, the pigment having penetrated the muscle before he grew fat. His chin was adorned with a false beard of horse hair, hanging from a strip and thickly and lumpily dyed with black. The embalming process is exactly as described by Herodotus. A bronze cauldron filled with large stones and seeds of charred hemp also bears out Herodotus' account of the Scythian inhaling of hashish for religious purposes.

In the fifth burial were some astonishing textiles. A deep red and yellow pile carpet 4 square metres in size

90 A bronze cauldron of Scythian type from the second tomb contained charred hemp-seeds and stones as mentioned in Herodotus

91 In the Pazyryk tombs of the High Altai appliqué work in brightly dyed felt is prominent. Here an eagle-griffin is represented attacking an ibex, which has the writhing action and impossible twist of the hindquarters which are also characteristic of the later Sarmatian art of Siberia

Ill. 92

and almost certainly Persian, was decorated with plant ornaments in the middle and with two bands of figures, the inner one a procession of stags, and the outer a procession of riders in hoods, tunics and tight trousers on horses with clipped manes and feather head-dresses. Among appliqué felt hangings two are pre-eminent. One

Ill. 98

shows a curious lion-bodied monster with wings, a human head, and antlers, fighting a fantastic giant bird.

Ill. 93

On the other a rider, wearing a short cloak and tight trousers and bareheaded, approaches a figure seated on a throne, shaven headed, wearing a fur cap and a long robe, while a 'tree of life' stands close by. A felt chariot-cover bears representations of tethered swans in Chinese style.

92, 93 The pile carpet, over 6 feet square, comes from the fifth tomb at Pazyryk. Representations of griffins next to a plant design in the centre and a procession of riders in hoods and tight trousers with a Central Asian look are main features. The weave and quality of the carpet are reckoned Persian. The felt hanging from the fifth tomb (right) is of great religious interest. It shows twice over the scene of a bare-headed horseman approaching the throne of a mysterious divine figure. The seated figure is now usually regarded as a form of the Great Goddess of the Near East (*cf. Ill. 57*). Her long tight robe in blue and brown, her tight fitting fur cap and the shape of her ear suggest China or at any rate the Far East

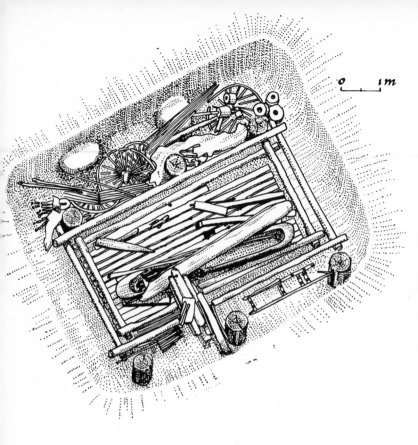

94 A view of the fifth tomb, showing, the timbered chamber and cross sections of the six posts which originally supported a hemp-smoking tent on its site. Inside the chamber are the coffins with their lids and small furnishings, outside at the top are the parts of a four-wheeled waggon, and also a carpet, felt hangings and a felt cover for the waggon. Outside at the bottom is another part of the waggon

95 A view of the burial in the fifth tomb. The frozen body of a man of European type with a large, narrow skull and a narrow arched nose is seen with hands across the breast. The population was still mainly of this type though mongoloids were infiltrating from the forests. This body also showed traces of tattooing

96 The dismantled waggon found in the fifth tomb is of light construction. Its width is 10 feet, its total height 9 feet and its wheels are 6 feet 6 inches in diameter. It has four wheels, a raised seat for the driver and a hood of black felt, decorated with felt cut-outs of Chinese style in the form of swans. Such vehicles were known later in China under the Han dynasty

97, 98 Among the saddle-cloths from Tomb 5 one shows long-robed women burning incense. They are presumably Persians and not nomads. A felt appliqué hanging from the same tomb (right), shows a mythical multi-coloured monster with a brown human face in combat with a fantastic bird

These finds show that the Scythian way of life was reproduced in full detail in at least one other region of the steppe and must have been well known to less fortunate hordes.

It is probably a mere accident of discovery that so few tombs of the Iranian nomads on this grand scale are known beside those of South Russia and Pazyryk. But some special link between the two regions is likely, for the resemblance between the artistic styles is so close. Yet there are certain differences; among the Scythians the strongest Near Eastern influences are Median, Urartian, and Mesopotamian, coming through the Caucasus but at Pazyryk these are overlaid by those of Achaemenid Persia of the succeeding period, which must have reached the Altai by way of Central Asia. It has already been noticed that Chinese influence replaces Greek so far east. There are also links with later Sarmatian art in the writhing posture of the attacked animals. So too at Bashadar in the Central Altai the wavy technique for representing tigers' stripes on a coffin-lid, and the style of depicting feathers on eagles, are much the same as in the Sarmatian plaques from Siberia, to be mentioned later.

Ills. 99–101

99 From the second barrow at Bashadar in the Central Altai comes this wooden coffin with a procession of tigers carved on its lid. The tigers are walking rather quietly for creatures of the Animal Style, but their prey has something of the usual contortion. There is a similar procession on the side. The style of the tigers prefigures some that appear in later Sarmatian goldwork

100 This gold aigrette in the form of a giant eagle holding a writhing ibex is Sarmatian work and closely resembles some objects from Bashadar. The frontal view and the style of the feathers and body are similar in both

101 This gilded eagle-griffin on a red felt background over wood is from the second barrow at Bashadar. It has strong affinities with later Sarmatian pieces

CHAPTER FIVE

The Nomads of Central Asia and the Sarmatians

The Nomads of Central Asia

Central Asia, to the north and north-east of Iran between the Caspian and the mountains of the Pamir Alai and western Tien Shan, and to the south of a line from the top of the Caspian to Lake Balkash, was the territory of other Iranian nomads whom it is convenient to call Sakas; this limited use of the term distinguishes them, though not rigidly, from the Sarmatians who are found farther north.

This territory was always distinguished from Iran proper by the Persians, and was divided by the Achaemenid kings into the satrapies of Chorasmia, Bactria and Sogdiana, with a fringe of nomads not under effective control. It consists of desert plains bordered on the east by mountains and crossed by two main rivers, the Oxus and the Jaxartes, now Amu Darya and Syr Darya, and marked by other watercourses and short rivers. Where the Oxus enters the Aral Sea there is marshy country, and elsewhere on its lower course there were for many centuries, extensive works of irrigation.

In the fertile areas the Chorasmian cultivators had walled cities often independent of the Achemenaids, while elsewhere the nomad Sakas wandered. The Sakas wore the usual nomad attire and used the usual gear, as may be seen from Persian reliefs. Their remains show that they imported deodar wood from the country south of the Hindu Kush, and arrows and beads from India and Mongolia. They had their own variety of the Animal Style. They were never subdued permanently even by the greatest Achaemenid kings. After Alexander the Great overthrew the Persian Empire the Chorasmians and Sakas together dominated the eastern steppes for a great distance, and left an enduring mark on the subsequent culture of the Sarmatians.

The Nomads between Central Asia and Mongolia

East of Central Asia, as defined, is a region which has critical importance for the later history of the nomads, namely Zungaria between the Tien Shan and the Altai, and beyond it the south-western part of the Gobi. South of the Tien Shan, the Tarim basin has much less importance because the way is largely barred by the Pamir. Through the small ranges and desert plain of Zungaria white nomads reached the borders of China at various times, as we saw, including not only Iranians but speakers of the Tocharian language who formed part of the composite horde called Yueh Chi by the Chinese historians.

The newcomers appear to have introduced the full technique of mounted nomadism among the tribes of Mongolia and Transbaikalia, who had previously been wandering herdsmen, keeping horses but seldom riding them. From Chinese records it appears that the nomads of the Gobi as late as the fifth century were still unmounted and easily defeated by charioteers. But by 300 BC they were expert cavalrymen whose methods the Chinese were obliged to copy in order to achieve any measure of success.

The Iranian nomads from the west seem also to have introduced the successive forms of the Animal Style and other kinds of nomad art, which are so closely copied by the Ordos bronzes of this region over some centuries, and reappear later among the textiles of Noin Ula, as will be seen.

The Sarmatians

An immense area of the steppes, stretching perhaps from Zungaria to Hungary, was at various times occupied or traversed by the Sarmatian peoples, who appeared in South Russia in the fourth century BC and continued to move westward through it for some seven hundred years until the end of the Roman Empire in the west. Before their great movements began, the most westerly of them was perhaps the tribe of the Sauromatae, which still lived east of the Don in the fifth century BC. To the east their original home is usually identified with the steppes on either side of the Volga between the Don and the Ural, but some of the tribes evidently wandered much farther east towards China.

At the southern end of the Ural mountains near Chkalov, a group of graves dated to the fifth and fourth centuries BC showed that at the time of the Scythian ascendancy in South Russia the Sarmatians buried their dead even more simply than the earliest Scythians. The tombs were shallow trenches, square, oval or circular, containing no wooden framework, and the bodies were not in coffins but simply wrapped in mantles of leather and fur. Arms, horse-trappings, garments, gold torques and pottery were found. There were no Greek imports, but there were some Persian silver cups and seals. Among weapons the Scytho-Median short sword, or akinakes, no longer appeared; there were short daggers of another kind, but much more prominent were long heavy lance-heads and long, double-edged, sharp-pointed swords.

The bow was less important, and so too were javelins and throwing spears. Armour consisted chiefly of corselets of linen or leather covered with scales of bone, bronze or even iron, such as were already known, but less common, among the Scythians. There were also conical helmets of bronze or iron. There was altogether more iron than with the Scythian remains, and here and there even heavy corselets of iron. In ornament the Animal Style was rare, a geometrical style with bright colours being preferred. Gold on quivers and sheaths and for ornaments was naturally not so common as in Scythian tombs. The graves of women yielded mirrors, earrings and other gear, and sometimes arrowheads. Horses were also occasionally buried.

Similar graves west of this area and in the delta of the Don contained the same objects, as well as a quantity of Greek objects, and had sometimes been roofed with flat beams. But the Sarmatians of this time did not yet build Royal Tombs.

At the eastern limit of their earliest territory the Sarmatians were in contact with the Chorasmians and Sakas of the Massagetic confederacy, to which some of their tribes were subject. The effects are manifest in the panoply described, which is that of heavy cavalry, invented in Central Asia and copied farther east and west. The use of leather foot thongs begins among these cavalry, who needed them to give a firmer seat to the mounted lancer, and so also does a new form of attack in close ranks of riders equivalent to a mounted phalanx. With such equipment and tactics the Sarmatians next drove the Royal Horde of Scythians of the Pontic Steppes into their later refuges in the Crimea and the Dobrudja. This manner of fighting was also adopted by the nomads of the Gobi and by the Chinese. It became characteristic of the whole Iranian world, both settled and nomadic, for some centuries.

102, 103   The Sarmatian torque ornament shown above is from an unknown site in Siberia. It is a figure in the round, representing a lion-griffin with cloisonné work on the mane, and with other large inlays. It has affinities with objects from the Oxus Treasure, such as the armlet (*Ill. 103*, opposite). Various objects of the Oxus Treasure represent a tradition, partly Persian and partly nomadic, with which the Sarmatians were in contact in their eastern territories. The gold armlet is an example of this with terminals shaped into two eagle-griffins with horns, their wings and necks inlaid with cloisonné work and their bodies bearing larger inlays

Sarmatian Art in Siberia

The same influence from Central Asia can be traced in Sarmatian art, which in its early phase had a polychrome Animal Style with jewelled inlays. The collection of Central Asian art of Achaemenid style which is known as the Oxus Treasure represents a tradition that must have been characteristic of Chorasmia and its vicinity during the fifth and fourth centuries B C. Among its favourite subjects are birds and beasts of prey and griffins, treated elaborately in styles which are nearly reproduced in Sarmatian goldwork from Siberia. Some of the personal ornaments carry gold griffins covered all over with cloisonné work, a technique reproduced in personal ornaments of the Sarmatians. A later technique of the Oxus Treasure, consisting of embossed relief only, with no more than vestigial inlay-sockets, is duly copied in Sarmatian belt-plates. Thus the earliest Sarmatian art

Ill. 102

Ill. 103

is now dated to the fifth and fourth centuries BC, and the next phase to the fourth and third.

To the second phase most authorities assign the remarkable gold plaques for belts, sheaths or quivers, which were plundered from unknown places in Siberia and saved by Peter the Great for the Siberian collection now kept in the Hermitage Museum at Leningrad. They show *Ills. 104, 107* violent combats, involving griffins, winged lions, serpents, tigers, wolves, eagles, elk, yak and other animals. They were executed in openwork, and some have a wavy lined style which recalls the coffin-lid from Bashadar in *Ill. 99* the Altai. Some represent human figures, such as horsemen hunting boar in wooded country, a mysterious *Ill. 105* reclining figure with his head on a woman's lap beside *Ill. 106* tethered horses, or again wrestlers between standing *Ill. 110* horses, all in a forest. These scenes seem to be distinctively Sarmatian, and may be taken from the life of 'The Great Hero of Middle Asia' as he has been called.

104–107 A typical piece of later Sarmatian art somewhere in western Siberia is this gold plaque (above) showing a fight between a tiger like those of Bashadar and an apparently horse-headed but carnivorous griffin with an ornamental bird-beak on his nose, and more on his mane and tail. This mixture of natural and supernatural was a favourite theme. A celebrated gold plaque in openwork (below) shows an exciting moment in a boar-hunt on the wooded edge of the Siberian Steppe. A Sarmatian rider, perhaps the hero who seems to be the subject of several of these plaques, pursues with drawn bow a powerful boar, from which another rider has taken refuge up a tree, with his horse apparently trying to climb up after him. The hair and moustache

of both men are in true Sarmatian style, like their equipment. The trees and their leaves are shown in characteristic manner. These forested scenes with strong indication of background seem to be specifically Sarmatian. Another plaque of this group (above) shows a man in a tight fitting tunic and trousers resting or lying dead on the lap of a woman who wears a curious high head-dress. The man's bowcase hangs on a tree, while a servant squats holding by reins two saddled horses with close-cropped manes and long tails. This may likewise be an incident in the life of the hero. A battle is shown on the Sarmatian gold plaque (below) between a wild animal with shortened legs and a serpent coiled round it. This theme is imitated on Ordos bronzes

108–110 The Ordos bronzes include plaques of contorted animal forms within the general shape of a horizontal B (*Ill. 108*), as among the Sarmatians. Sarmatian inspiration is evident in the Ordos openwork plaque (*Ill. 109*), showing a tiger devouring a ram. *Ill. 110*, left, an Ordos bronze *c.* 100 BC–AD 100, represents two men of Sarmatian, not mongoloid, appearance wrestling in a forest between two horses

Ills. 108, 109

The designs of the Sarmatian gold plaques are so closely reproduced in some of the later Ordos bronzes of North China and the Gobi that direct copying seems certain. Other late Ordos bronzes show a strong Chinese influence, but their conception and fundamental style remain Sarmatian in this sense as is particularly evident in many of the animal shapes and forms.

The Sarmatians in South Russia and Eastern Europe

Driven from the east, the Sarmatians crossed the Don in force late in the fourth century BC. One of their tribes, the Siraci, occupied the Kuban shortly before 300 BC, and remained there for five centuries; others, such as the Jazyges, Urgi, and Roxolani, occupied the Pontic Steppe from 300 to 100 BC and then passed up the Danube,

Ill. 111

where the Romans knew them for centuries more. During the second century BC the Saii and later, perhaps from

111, 112   A scene on Trajan's column gives the clearest picture known of the Sarmatian panoply of scale-armour for man and horse. Swords and bows are shown, but not the usual long heavy lances, probably dropped in flight. The riders apparently are not equipped with leather thongs in which to place their feet and neither is anything shown of their saddles and girths. The Sarmatians used a curious system of signs carved on stones (*Ill. 112*) or other objects and remotely descended from the Bosporan Greek alphabet. The signs had a long development as is seen on this inscribed stone from Krivoi Rog, which was used for centuries and has signs running over one another. *Tamgas*, as they are called, were emblems of ruling clans among the Sarmatians

125–61 BC, the Royal Sarmatians established their rule over other tribes west of the Dniepr. From the east after 100 BC the Aorsi and then the Alani forced their way westward to overthrow the Royal Sarmatians. On the Pontic Steppes and even more in Hungary the Sarmatians were continually in contact with the Thracian, Celtic and German tribes, who were not nomads. The dominant tribe did not always expel the others, but must have permitted them to dwell round the territory as subjects. It has been argued that some Slavonic tribes at this time had Sarmatian rulers.

The Sarmatians succeeded the Scythians as customers of the Greek traders, showing particular respect for the half-Greek kingdom of Bosporus in the eastern Crimea and the Taman Peninsula. The culture of Bosporus and of other Greek cities outside it never ceased to be Greek in some sense until the Pontic Sarmatians were overrun by the Goths from the north-west.

Ill. 112

113 The animals represented on this gold scent-bottle from Novocherkassk near the mouth of the Don are in Central Asian or Siberian Animal style with large inlay-hollows

The later history of the Sarmatians, as known from classical sources, is one of increasing pressure in South Russia, and of increasing flow into the Danube valley, where they were continually fighting the Roman armies until their unrest culminated in the great disturbance of the Hunnish advance.

Later Sarmatian Art

From the third century BC onward the burials and gear of the Sarmatian princes and nobles, male and female, became more elaborate in all the areas mentioned. ·

For example, near Novocherkassk on the lower Don one of a large group of barrows yielded the skeleton of a woman buried with some elaborate goldwork. The principal find was a diadem in the shape of a gold band; along the top were figures of stags with rings in their mouths walking among trees, all very much in the manner of the Siberian plaques, and two birds like geese; in the middle were set large amethysts and garnets and the bust of a crowned woman in chalcedony, while figures of birds of prey were set between the great jewels, and from the lower edge hung pendants in the form of little amphorae. The diadem no doubt held on a head-cloth or a veil.

35267

114   The treasure of the barrow called Khoklach at Novocherkassk is the best-known group of
Sarmatian finds in South Russia. It was found in the grave of a woman, probably a queen of the
Aorsi, of the first or second century A D. On the diadem shown here the animal figures at the top
are like those found much farther east, including some of the Ordos region. The Aorsi came from
the eastern edge of Central Asia. The style of the trees has the same affinities. The collar or
coronet is a true example of Sarmatian Animal Style, being encrusted with coral and topaz, using
red and black inlay for the eyes. The animal forming the handle of the cup might equally be a
deer or an elk. A needle-box and a perfume-box covered in intricate repoussé decoration are
also shown

115, 116 In the centre of this large silver *phalera* with embossed gold leaf from the Sadovy barrow at Novocherkassk is a scene of a griffin attacking a panther. It is in a crowded Sarmatian style with encrustations of semi-precious stones. Stylized panthers surround the central scene and twenty birds' heads adorn the rim. The silver bowl (right) has very elaborate feather-ornament on the inner surface, and is also gilded. The central scene is a satirical one of a wine-harvest; a harvester arrives with three baskets, but a Silenus in a tree will not let him gather the grapes and pushes a basket down on his head. Purely Greek work

Ills. 113, 114   There were also a gold collar in openwork decorated with friezes of griffins above and below; a gold scent-bottle and a circular box, both decorated in repoussé with beasts in the Animal Style; a gold cup with a handle in the form of a deer, and minor finds too numerous to mention. This is believed to have been the grave of a queen, according to some, of the second century AD, but perhaps older.

Another royal burial of the same group was in a pit covered with planks. It yielded circular phalarae of silver
Ill. 115   covered with embossed gold leaf showing a griffin
Ills. 116–118   attacking a panther, eight Hellenistic silver wine bowls, decorated in the centre with medallions in relief showing scenes of Greek myth, all under a silver washing bowl.
Ill. 119   Also two bronze cauldrons covered with soot, in which the funeral feast had evidently been cooked, as well as a bronze vase and an amphora which had held the wine.

117-119 Eight silver bowls from which probably the Sarmatian nobles drank at the funeral feast were found in the Sadovy barrow. The bowl above has a feather plant ornament, and in the centre a Nereid riding on a hippocamp, a sea monster with horse's forequarters. *Ill. 118* above, right, has Cupid fettered to a column, while Psyche presses a burning torch to his body and a figure of Nemesis stands by on a raised base. A cauldron (*Ill. 119*) from the same burial, one of two, is a typically nomad vessel such as was used everywhere on the steppes at the time

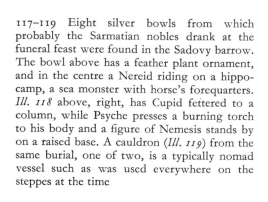

This barrow is approximately of the same date as the other previously mentioned.

Such burials confirm that the Sarmatian chiefs and their wives on the Pontic Steppe were on the same terms with the Greeks as the Scythians had been, and that they too built Royal Tombs. Even more like Scythian burials were four barrows excavated at Jasz Also Szent György in Hungary. The largest covered a wooden chamber in

120, 121 From the Zubov barrow near Anapa on the eastern shore of the Black Sea comes the gold ornament of the first or second century AD showing two stages of a victorious beheading. First the defeated enemy is seized; then the victor drags his headless body with one hand and carries his head in the other. The head was perhaps intended to be presented to the king as evidence of prowess. The Sarmatian plaque (*Ill. 121*) from Kurdzhips in the Kuban is of the third century BC. Two victors appear, one holding the severed head, the other the sword used

which lay the skeleton of a Sarmatian prince along with the remains of a funeral car, skeletons of horses and treasure. The others contained the remains of his retinue, including those of beheaded warriors. The burials were dated to the third century AD.

Ills. 120, 121, 123

Ills. 122, 124–129

Gilded silver phalerae of a special Sarmatian type have been found at such places as Szörcse in Transylvania, Herastrau near Bucharest and Galiche in Bulgaria. They show the same style as others from Yanchokrak Starobielsk and Taganrog in South Russia. They have representations of men, some of them riding, and in one case of a woman with thick plaits, all dressed in the same

122, 123 This large *phalera*, or round horse-trapping, of gilded silver from an unknown place on the coast of the Black Sea is typical of these ornaments found in South Russia or on the Danube. In the centre an animal which may be a wolverine devours an antelope; round the edge two winged wolf-like monsters with bushy tails pursue a leopard, and two eagle-griffins appear on either side of an ox-head. *Ill. 123*, below, a gilded fibula from Maikop, shows, in the round, a Sarmatian brandishing a severed head

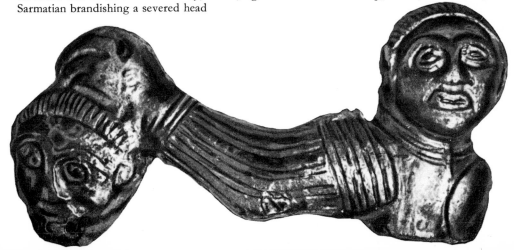

124–127 A silver *phalera* from Herastrau, Rumania, above, shows the heavy quilted jacket or tunic that the Sarmatians often wore, no doubt against the cold. To the right another *phalera* from Galiche, Bulgaria shows the Great Goddess, her hair in heavy plaits, with sacred birds, perhaps ravens, on her shoulders and heavy pleated dress. Two other *phalerae* from Galiche (below) are ornamented with designs of Iranian origin, petal-shaped (left) and large similar plant ornament (right)

128–130 From Surcea, or Szörcse, in Transylvania the oval *phalera* (above, left) shows a Sarmatian rider with long sword and dog (as on some Siberian plaques). Above his head is an eagle, which should be a symbol of divine favour, or an embodiment of some helping spirit. Another Sarmatian rider on a round *phalera* from Galiche wears a heavy long cloak with a high collar. From their position his feet might be in leather loops. The style of these western *phalerae* shows a certain amount of Greek influences. The broad-topped fibula from Transylvania (*Ill. 130*) shows an unusually broad human face. Fibulae imply cloaks, which may be a sign of western influence

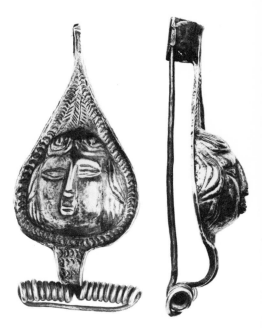

thickly pleated costume. It is thought that they were made for the Sarmatian market by Greeks, probably at Olbia. Beads and small ornaments of the Danubian Sarmatians show that some imports came through the Pontic cities from Transcaucasia, Western Asia, and even India.

Ill. 130

107

131   Map of the Sarmatian, Saka and Hunnish movements of the fourth century BC to

the fifth century AD

CHAPTER SIX

The Nomads of the East and the Huns

Nomad Movements in the East

Beyond the Sarmatians, in Central Asia and farther east, movements of great historical importance began during the same period. Not all of them ended as merely barbarian migrations or invasions, but some founded civilized states.

The first dynasty to be founded directly by mounted nomads was the Parthian dynasty of Iran, founded by the brothers Arsaces and Tiridates, leaders of the Parni, Sakas who came into northern Iran from the steppe between the Caspian and the Aral about 250 BC. The Parthians gradually overcame the Seleucid successors of Alexander and ruled a large empire until they were overthrown by Ardashir Papakan, founder of the Sassanid dynasty, in AD 224. Though they were always regarded as aliens, the Parthians protected the centre of Iran from later nomad invasions and fought, often successfully, against the Romans.

Farther east the Greek kingdom of Bactria, which likewise began in a rebellion against the Seleucids, was less fortunate. On its original territory it lasted for something more than a century, while its later kings extended their rule into northern India, where a fragment of it survived as late as 55 BC. The original kingdom of Bactria was struck down by a nomad invasion from the north. This movement was part of a chain of events which affected the entire extent of the northern steppes, and which must now be described.

Ill. 131

The Hsiung Nu, the Yueh Chi and the Sakas

The origin of this great disturbance was in the rapid growth of the Hsiung Nu power among the nomads of the Gobi. By the end of the third century BC the Hsiung Nu, who are first mentioned in Chinese annals at this time, had formed a confederacy which dominated the western Gobi and for a long time fought on equal terms with the Han Dynasty of China. This empire, which was like the Scythian dominion of South Russia, was in direct contact with the Chinese over a long frontier in the region where the Great Wall had been built to hold such nomads in check. Its expert cavalry improved on the Sarmatian style of fighting by adopting an extremely powerful reflex bow, stiffened at the ends with plates of bone, which in its earliest form appears to have been invented by hunting tribes round Lake Baikal before 500 BC. This bow became the regular weapon of mounted nomad conquerors from the eastern steppes over many centuries.

The Hsiung Nu reached their greatest power under the chief Mao-tun early in the second century BC. Mao-tun inflicted a crushing defeat on the horde immediately to the west, the Yueh Chi, who had once been stronger. The resulting Yueh Chi migration was the beginning of many troubles in Central Asia. The Yueh Chi appear to have been a composite horde, in which a royal tribe of Iranians ruled over subject tribes of Tocharians and perhaps over some Turks. After their king had been killed in another attack, they fled westward through Zungaria to the Upper Ili valley about 160 BC. There they were attacked and driven westward by another horde, the Wu Sun, allied to the Hsiung Nu, passed south westward into Sogdiana, and eventually moved into Bactria about 100 BC. Of the Saka peoples, whom they displaced, some entered Parthia and by mixing with the previous inhabitants formed the Pahlava people who conquered part of western India. Others migrated directly south to found the Saka kingdoms of India. In Bactria the Yueh Chi destroyed the Greek cities and settled the country in five districts. The ruler of one district, Kujula Kadphises, made himself king over the whole country, and then with his son made wide conquests in India, overcoming the Pahlavas and Sakas there. Thus was founded the Kushan Empire, which at its height ruled northern India and much of Central Asia, and was in contact with the Han in the Tarim basin. Before its power was broken by the Sassanids in the third century AD, it had transmitted Buddhism to China.

The Hsiung Nu and the Huns

The empire of the Hsiung Nu continued for some centuries as a rival to the Han Empire of China. At its widest it extended from Korea to the Altai and from the Chinese border to Transbaikalia. It developed an elaborate system of government under its supreme ruler the Shanyü. According to Chinese historians there were two great divisions of territory, the eastern and western, administered by a hierarchy known as the twenty-four leaders, who controlled many subject tribes. They carried out an annual census of all livestock in the empire. For burial they used elaborate double coffins with accessories of gold and fur, but built no grave-mounds. In true nomad fashion they slaughtered the favourite ministers and concubines of a dead Shanyü to accompany him along with thousands of humbler followers and buried also his personal belongings.

Han diplomacy worked to divide the Hsiung Nu and win over individual chiefs, until during the first century AD the Hsiung Nu were finally divided into a southern group under varying degrees of Chinese control and a northern group, which was independent, but was steadily worn down by the attacks of the southern group and of other nomads instigated by the Chinese. The northern Hsiung Nu were overthrown altogether in the second century AD by the Sien Pi, another horde, but as late as AD 311, after the fall of the Han, a band of southern Hsiung Nu destroyed the northern capital Lo Yang. An outlying group, which had migrated west in 50 BC to cause much trouble in Central Asia, had been destroyed before 30 BC by a Chinese expedition.

We come now to a much disputed question of the Hsiung Nu and the Huns, who are often regarded as the same people. It is not likely that any cohesive horde of Hsiung Nu remained in Central Asia to become the ancestors of the Huns, but some clans of survivors may have mingled with Iranian nomads and also with mongoloids from the northern forests to form a new people, the Huns.

Chinese sources report that the Hsiung Nu were hairy and had prominent noses. European sources give a prevailing impression that the Huns were Mongoloid. The Ephthalite kings who appear in Indian history as Hunas and are represented on coins, are not shown as mongoloid. It can only be concluded that the Huns in Central Asia were a mixed people, not even uniformly mixed, of whom those who invaded Europe were more mongoloid than the rest. In Eastern Asia the ruling Hsiung Nu have not yet been traced archaeologically with any certainty, but remains of the Huns can now be identified westward from Central Asia far into Europe. On the linguistic side we have almost no remains of the Hunnish language in Europe, but the Ephthalites, or

White Huns, appear to have spoken a Turkish language, and Hsiung Nu words and phrases preserved in Chinese sources are considered by some authorities to belong at least to an Altaic language.

The Tombs of Noin Ula

Though archaeology has not traced the Hsiung Nu, one people of northern Mongolia which should have been among their subjects has left remains surpassed only in South Russia and the Altai. In the Noin Ula mountains on the Selenga river, which flows into Lake Baikal, are three groups of barrows, numbering 212 in all. They are dated from the first century BC onward. In barrows opened so far the timbers and the unplundered contents were preserved by water, which had leaked in immediately and never dried. The tombs were in rectangular trenches with flights of steps leading down to the bottom.

Ill. 132

Each burial chamber consisted of an outer room, more than 5 metres long and two-thirds as wide and one-third as high, walled and roofed with logs, the roof being also supported with pillars of timber. Inside this was a smaller chamber more than 3 metres long with width and height in the same proportion, also pillared, in which lay a carefully carpentered wooden coffin. The bodies, which were sometimes of European type, were elaborately dressed, and remains of sacrifices were still spread about the graves. The walls, roofs and floors were covered with silk, felt, and woollen stuffs, mostly very well preserved. There were no bones of horse-sacrifices and none of slaughtered retainers or concubines.

The most remarkable finds came from the sixth of the excavated barrows. An embroidered felt carpet had Chinese designs in the middle and round the edge, and in between a repeated design of two animal combats separated by Trees of Life, a yak butting against a horned lion and a lion-griffin springing upon an elk from the

Ill. 133

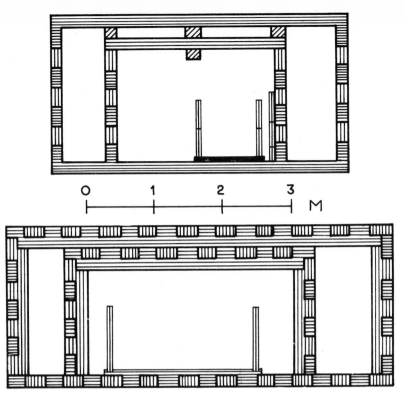

O 1 2 3 M

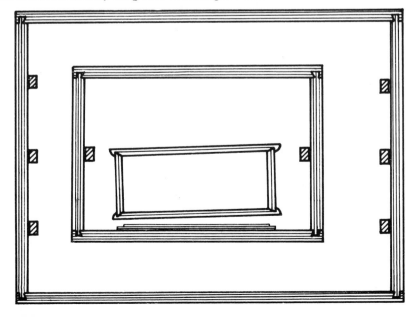

132 Plan and sections of the sixth barrow at Noin Ula on the Selenga river, showing the outer and inner chamber with the coffin. The barrow perhaps dates from the first century BC. The sides of the barrow were originally walled with stone-work. Many scholars assume that such barrows as this are actually the graves of Hsiung Nu chiefs

133 A scene of combat in the typical Animal Style appears on this felt carpet. The inspiration is Sarmatian; the griffin appears to be a lion-griffin but might also be a winged wolverine. The victim is clearly an elk from its muzzle and horns. Though these animals are in nomad style the yak and lion shown elsewhere on this hanging are more in Chinese style. They recall the animal combats seen on the Pazyryk tapestries, *Ill. 91*

Ill. 134

Ill. 135

rear. These were in the nomad Animal Style. One wall-hanging was embroidered with tigers' heads in purely Chinese style; another with a design of tortoises and fishes among water plants, and a third with birds and fishes in water. The last two have been compared to Greek adornments found on walls and ceilings of a Roman villa of approximately the same date. There were also three pairs of baggy Chinese trousers, two long-sleeved women's dresses, one of silk and the other a warm one of felt with silk ornamentation, a silk bonnet, a fur bonnet, and plaits of women's hair, some in sheaths,

134 The design of this wall-hanging from the sixth barrow consists of tortoises and fishes in frames of stylized water-plants. The whole hanging is of woollen fabric, now reddish-brown, but once perhaps purple. Heart-shaped flowers and trefoils with tendrils form squares in which are framed the shapes of tortoises and stylized fishes. Each tortoise holds blades of grass in its mouth. Both fishes and tortoises vary slightly in pattern

probably funeral offerings in place of slaughtered women. Two silver plaques bore designs of yaks on rocks among trees somewhat in Sarmatian style. *Ill. 136*

In the twenty-fifth barrow were remains of a wall-hanging embroidered with two life-like moustached men's faces of western type, recalling another hanging in the sixth barrow which shows the figures of two riders, recognizably Scythian in type. Some authorities regard these hangings as imports by way of the steppes from South Russia, others as Graeco-Syrian work with nomad themes, imported through Iran. In any case, these *Ill. 137*

135, 136   The Chinese clothes opposite come from the sixth barrow at Noin Ula. The bonnet is lined with silk covered with sable fur and equipped with streamers. The trousers are of woollen fabric and dark purple. Round the hem at the waist is a thick woollen cord. The trousers were held up with a belt and adorned with bands of coloured wool. The long silk coat is now of a sandy colour but was once ruby; it is 1·17 metres long and 1·94 metres between sleeve-tips, and is trimmed with sable. From the sixth barrow again is a silver plaque (above) showing a yak standing on rocks among fir-trees on a mountain. The yak is represented on Sarmatian plaques, but not with this frontal pose of the head combined with the body in profile. This must be due to another influence. The animal's feet have little relation to the ground on which it stands far western connections are as clearly attested as the Chinese, and are evidence for no mean sophistication on the northern edge of the Gobi.

At Ulan Ude, where the Ivolga flows into the Selenga, were traces of a large fortified settlement of many houses, which had flues for hot air and smoke under their floors as in Roman hypocaustic heating. It is quite likely that this form of heating was independently invented by the Chinese. The settlement may have been built for the Hsiung Nu by transported Chinese workers, and could have been garrisoned with Chinese prisoners of war under Hsiung Nu officers, as a fort against the tribes of the northern forests. It seems soon to have been destroyed. The relation of nomad to cultivator and even townsman was no less complex in the Far East than in Chorasmia or South Russia.

The Advance of the Huns

The advance of the Huns from Central Asia, which shook but did not destroy the Sassanian power in Iran, penetrated into India, and struck deep into Europe, precipitating the end of the West Roman Empire.

The earliest mention of the Huns in Classical writers is thought to be a reference in Ptolemy's *Geography*, a little later than AD 150 to a people called Chuni, apparently on the Caucasian Steppe. This seems to be confirmed by Armenian sources, admittedly much later than the events, which report Hunnish raids from this quarter into western Iran early in the third century AD. Otherwise western sources say nothing of the Huns until they appear in force in the years following AD 370 to destroy the Gothic power in South Russia.

In Central Asia the Ephthalites occupied the former Kushan territory and fought the Sassanid kings of Iran continually during the fifth and sixth centuries, even intervening in dynastic struggles. For some thirty years

137 In the twenty-fifth barrow of Noin Ula pieces of a wall-hanging showed human faces of western aspect, rather broad and square and apparently of the Armenoid type represented among the Iranian nomads. This hanging recalls another from the sixth barrow where two riders of the same race appear. These hangings may have come from South Russia and may represent Scythians such as still survived in the Crimea

from AD 500 western India too was ruled by Hun kings belonging to the same people.

But it is the Western, or Black Huns, who are best known to history from the accounts of Greek and Roman writers such as Ammianus, Priscus and Procopius. The Hunnish king Balamber destroyed the Ostrogothic

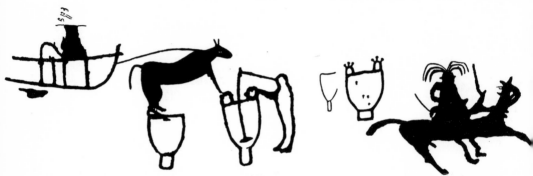

138   This rock carving from Kizil Kaya on the river Uibat in southern Siberia probably shows Hunnish life of the second and third century A D. On the left an animal that may be a hornless ox draws a sledge. Two wild riders with feathered head-dresses set the tone for the scene which seems to be a religious rite. Five sacred cauldrons are in use; their contents are stirred or pounded with long rods which have flat spreading tips. Such cauldrons are known from Hunnish sites

kingdom between the Don and the Dniestr in A D 376. The Visigoths west of the Dniestr were next overwhelmed. The Sarmatians of South Russia now passed back under nomad rule. Goths fleeing before the Huns were allowed to cross the Danube into the Balkan provinces where the Roman authorities hoped to make use of them eventually as settlers. The Huns, now in command of the Alani and other Sarmatians, advanced into the Danube valley, and, without losing their control of South Russia or of countries farther east, made their headquarters in Hungary for operations against the Roman Empire. Their armies under Octar and Rua made great raids into the Balkan

139 Two chiefs' golden bows from Hunnish sites. On the right are the plates and the reconstruction of the smaller symbolic bow from Jakuszowice, which has no stiffening plates of bone, and, to judge from the shape of the gold plates, was permanently bent. Below are the gold plates alone on a larger bow from Pecsüszög, which appears to have been a real weapon not gilded on its bending parts. From the remains accompanying each, other differences are inferred. The chief buried at Jakuszowice was a native who held authority from the Huns; hence he had a golden bow, but only silver-plated harness. The other is likely to have been a Hun, since his harness too was gilded

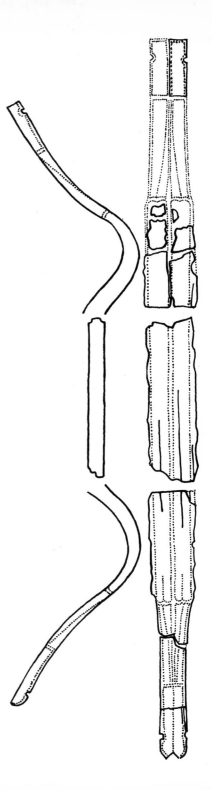

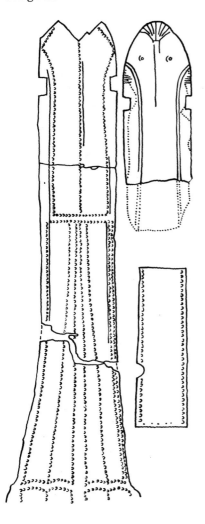

provinces and extorted large sums of tribute in gold coin. Sometimes the Romans, like the Sassanids, took Huns into service as cavalry and even used them against rebels.

The Empire of Attila

When they first reached the Danube valley, the Huns were still a confederacy of their own tribes, with Sarmatian tribes under rule; to these they began to add non-nomadic German tribes. But they did not have a unified state until this was created for his lifetime by Attila in A D 434.

Attila began to change the confederacy into an empire ruled by himself through a new order of grandees. The grandees were not all of Hunnish origin; many appear to have been Germans, and there may also have been Sarmatians and even Slavs. They were often ruling chiefs in their own right, but were not necessarily so, and owed their special powers and status to their position in Attila's service. But at the same time Attila continued to rule directly over his own Huns, of all social classes, with their own horses and cattle. Without this military and economic base his power as an overlord would soon have become merely nominal.

Ill. 138

His system of grandees has been compared to that of the contemporary Sassanids, about whom he must have been informed. Through it he ruled an immense territory north of the Danube in Europe as far as the Baltic, and also the Eurasian Steppes at least as far as the Caspian. He raided not only the Balkan provinces of the Roman Empire but also Gaul in 451 and Italy north of the Apennines in 453. His sudden death in A D 453 forestalled a grand attack on the East Roman Empire, and brought his system and the unified power of the Huns to a premature end. The Hunnish Empire was broken up by dynastic quarrels and rebellion of the subject peoples, particularly the Germans.

140 This gold diadem from a grave at Karagalik in the Tien Shan, perhaps of the second century A D, is adorned with figures in Chinese style and may be Chinese work. Below flying geese, winged bird-women gallop by; one on a lion-dragon, one on an ibex, one on a buffalo, and below these, one on a winged lion, passing various animals. They are interpreted on Chinese analogies as fairies making their way through the other world. The grave may be that of a female shaman of the Huns

Before and under Attila the Hunnish dominion consisted of central territories held by the Huns in varying strength, and a ring of lands occupied by subject peoples under obedient chiefs or Hunnish governors. Archaeology has revealed fairly clear traces of Hunnish rule. Burials of local chiefs in the outlying regions have yielded, among more usual treasures and weapons, a number of gold plates of curious shape. It is now believed that they were gilding plates for ceremonial bows which would have been emblems of Hunnish authority. Some of the bows were evidently of full size and their plates would have been applied only to the unbending middle section; these could have been real weapons, however ornate. Others were smaller and must, from the shape of the plates, have been gilded from end to end; these would have been purely ceremonial objects. Such bow-plates have been found for example at Pecsüszög in Hungary, Jakuszowice in Poland, and far away east at such places as Novogrigoryevko on the Dniepr and

Ill. 139

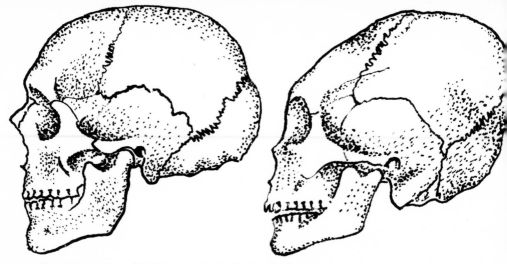

141 The deformation of skulls found in barbarian burials of the Hunnish period is illustrated by this comparison of two skulls. The normal skull on the left is from Heilbronn, the deformed one on the right from Niederolm, both in Germany. The custom spread from the east to the Sarmatians and Germans, and is found in skulls of this period as far as Korea

Ill. 140

Ill. 141

Borovoye on the Tobol in North Kazakhstan. Distinctively Hunnish diadems, cylindrical cauldrons, mirrors, gold-plated belts, and long single-edged cavalry sabres have a similar distribution. More widespread are the artificially rounded skulls of Hunnish and kindred burials between Central Europe and Central Asia.

Conclusion

The history of the steppes has now been carried to a decisive point, the end of the ancient period of Indo-European nomadism. The advance of the Huns was the beginning of the second age of mounted nomads, dominated by Altaic peoples, which continues through the Dark and Middle Ages of European history and far into the modern period. China, Central Asia and Eastern Europe were invaded by one after another of these people from the eastern steppes in a series culminating in the Mongol conquests. It is only in our own time that the Russian and Chinese states between them have very nearly made an end of nomadism over the whole of this immense region.

Chronology

I 4000–2000 B C. Origin and Rise of Pastoral Societies

A SOUTH RUSSIA   Neolithic culture of mixed farming, followed by Copper Age, on the steppe, *Tripolye* culture with painted pottery in phases; A *c.* 3800–3500; BI *c.* 3500–3200; BII *c.* 3200–2800; CI *c.* 2800–2500; CII *c.* 2500–2000 or later. Similar cultures in the Danube valley over these centuries. *Usatovo* culture of increasingly pastoral character contemporary with late *Tripolye* to the south-east. Beginning of pastoral societies in North Caucasia and in Pontic Steppe. Growth of Indo-European languages in this region from *c.* 2500. Waggons begin to be used on the steppe toward 2000.

B CAUCASIA AND THE NEAR EAST   North of the Caucasus, mixed farming and the beginning of pastoral societies as in South Russia. Copper Age with Mesopotamian influence. From *c.* 2300 BC, *Nalchik, Maikop* and similar burials. Hittites and kindred peoples reach Anatolia about 2000 BC, probably by way of Caucasus. Later, contact between North Caucasia and the Near East ceases.

C KAZAKHSTAN AND WESTERN SIBERIA   Neolithic mixed farming. Mongoloids in forests, whites on steppes. *Afanasyevo* culture on Siberian Steppe develops into pastoral phase between 3000 and 1700, Copper Age in later phases.

D CENTRAL ASIA, ZUNGARIA, PAMIR, TURKESTAN, ARAL REGION   Neolithic mixed farming except in mountains and deserts. Near Merv, *Anau* culture in phases: I *c.* 3400–2000; II *c.* 2600–2200; III *c.* 2200–2000. *Kelteminar* culture in Aral region *c.* 2800–2000. Copper Age.

E ALTAI, UPPER YENISEI, TARIM BASIN   Before 3000, mesolithic culture, then neolithic stone technique but little or no agriculture. Mongoloids in forests, whites on steppes, mongoloids again in habitable parts of Tibet.

F FAR EAST   Before 3000, mesolithic culture in north. *Serovo* culture of hunters and fishers in Siberia *c.* 3000–2500, followed by *Kitoi* culture 2500–2000. Neolithic cultures in North China with crude grey pottery.

II 2000–1500 B C. Spread of Pastoral Societies

A SOUTH RUSSIA   End of *Tripolye* culture soon after 2000. Increase of pastoral nomadism. Indo-European peoples increasingly active and spreading with flocks and waggons. Beginnings of Bronze Age Catacomb graves on Pontic Steppe from 2000.

B CAUCASIA, ETC.   Bronze Age. Indic branch of Indo-Europeans crosses Caucasus to Iran and Near East and introduces light horse-drawn chariots for war. Iranian branch remains north of Caucasus. *Kuban-Terek* culture in North Caucasia and on Caucasian Steppe. North Caucasian dolmens towards 1500. In Transcaucasia local cultures influenced from Anatolia and Near East, such as that of *Trialeti*, flourish from *c.* 1500. In Anatolia, rise of Hittite power. In North Mesopotamia and Syria, rise of Mitannian power under Indic rulers. Riding for war comes slowly into use in Near East.

C KAZAKHSTAN, ETC.   Bronze Age from *c.* 1750. *Andronovo* culture on steppes with mixed farming from *c.* 1750 BC.

D CENTRAL ASIA, ETC.   Bronze Age from *c.* 1750 in north, earlier in south. *Andronovo* culture in north.

E ALTAI, ETC.   Bronze Age as above. *Andronovo* culture in Minusinsk region.

F FAR EAST   From *c.* 2000 BC. *Yang Shao* culture with painted pottery on Upper Hwang Ko. *Lung Shan* culture with polished black pottery farther east. About 1500 BC, Bronze Age, Shang state founded in Hwang Ho valley uses the war-chariot.

III 1500–1000 BC. Beginnings of Mounted Nomadism

A SOUTH RUSSIA   Cimmerians; after *c.* 1250 dominant on Pontic Steppe, as they develop mounted nomadism. Mounted nomadism an established way of life towards 1000 BC.

B CAUCASIA, ETC.   Riding for war becoming commoner in Near East, but charioteering still dominant until *c.* 1200. Hittite Empire in Anatolia and North Syria until *c.* 1200. Hittite monopoly of iron ends with fall of Empire, and Iron Age begins in Near East generally. Iranians from *c.* 1000 begin to spread southward through Caucasia to northern Iran. Mounted nomadism established on Caucasian Steppe towards 1000 BC.

C KAZAKHSTAN, ETC.   Late *Andronovo* culture on steppes. Indo-Europeans begin to spread as nomads eastward through northern steppes towards 1000 BC. End of *Andronovo* culture.

D CENTRAL ASIA, ETC.   *Karasuk* culture of Chinese affinities succeeds *Andronovo* culture in eastern parts of this region about 1100.

E ALTAI, ETC.   Eastern *Andronovo* culture continues until *c.* 1100, when mongoloids perhaps from the border of North China arrive in sufficient numbers to introduce *Karasuk* culture, more pastoral and less agricultural.

F FAR EAST   From *c.* 1150 north-westward migration of mainly pastoral tribes from North China into Siberia, perhaps carrying with them Chinese types of knives and other articles, through *Ordos* region to Mongolia and Siberia. Shang state which perhaps caused *Karasuk* migration gives way to Chou Dynasty in 1027.

IV 1000–500 BC. Full Development of Mounted Nomadism on the Western Steppes

A SOUTH RUSSIA   Cimmerians dominate on Pontic Steppe until *c.* 750. Timber graves on Volga Steppe *c.* 900–800, probably those of earliest Scythian mounted nomads. Scythians move westward from Volga under Sarmatian pressure from the east. Some reach Transcaucasia, but the main body presses into Pontic Steppe to drive out Cimmerians into Danube valley, Crimea and Caucasia. Scythians pursue Cimmerians into Near East. After domination there, Scythians return to South Russia. Scythian burials in *Kuban* and then on Pontic Steppe. Scythians spread into Danube valley and parts of North European plain. Scythian contacts with Greeks in South Russia began in seventh century. Royal Scythians hold Empire on Pontic Steppe. Scythian Animal Style in South Russia. Darius I of Persia fails to destroy Scythian power in 513.

B CAUCASIA, ETC.   From *c.* 1000 to *c.* 750, *Koban* culture, perhaps Cimmerian, in northern Caucasia and astride the centre of the Caucasus. *Gandsha-Karabagh* culture in Transcaucasia and *Talysh* culture in Azerbaidjan show affinities with earlier stages of *Luristan* culture in the Zagros mountains of western Iran. Caucasian styles 750–650 may be forerunners of Scythian Animal Style. Cimmerians cross central Caucasus to devastate Urartu, threaten Assyria, and overrun Phrygia, Lydia and Greek cities of coast; also penetrate into Zagros mountains where they join the Medes. Scythians cross Caucasus at eastern end invade Urartu and occupy Azerbaidjan, perhaps 652–625. *Ziwiye* Treasure. Medes drive Scythians back over Caucasus. Fall of Assyria in 612 to Medes. Median Empire. Persian Empire founded by Cyrus the Great in 549.

C KAZAKHSTAN, ETC.   End of *Andronovo* culture after 1000, Pontic–Tocharian migration eastward across steppes in tenth century? Mounted nomadism spreads across western Siberia and Kazakhstan. Beginning of Sarmatian nomads, who are apparently checked eastward, but westward attack Scythians in eighth century.

D CENTRAL ASIA, ETC.   Iranians coming through Iran form settled culture in Chorasmia *c.* 700. Saka peoples appear north-east of Iran as mounted nomads and enemies of Persians. Cyrus the Great fails to subdue Massagetae beyond the Oxus in 530.

E ALTAI, ETC. Mounted nomads dominant on steppe by Altai mountains and Minusinsk *c.* 800. *Karasuk* culture disappears. *Maiemir* culture in Altai, *Tagar* culture in Minusinsk, corresponding to Scythic culture in South Russia with very similar Animal Style. Some mongoloid peoples begin to take up mounted nomadism. Earlier tombs of *Pazyryk* and *Bashadar* in Altai.

F FAR EAST   Sarmatian peoples on the edge of *Kansu* in north-west China. Also *Yueh Chi* under Iranian leadership. First spread of Animal Style into Mongolia and *Ordos*; earliest *Ordos* bronzes. Some mongoloid peoples north of China beginning to take up mounted nomadism about 500.

V   500 B C–0. Full Development of Mounted Nomadism on the Eastern Steppe among Non-Indo-European Peoples

A SOUTH RUSSIA   Scythian Empire at its height until *c.* 300; thereafter yields to Sarmatian pressure from the east. Rich Scythian burials continue on the *Dniepr* but cease in the *Kuban*, which is occupied by Sarmatians. Greatest Greek influence on Scythians. More Scythians spread into Danube valley, and after 300 Scythians increasingly concentrate in Crimea. After 250 Sarmatians dominant over the whole Pontic Steppe and pressing on into Danube valley among Thracians and Celts. Burials of *Novocherkassk* and *phalerae* of South Russia and Danube valley towards the end of this period.

B CAUCASUS, ETC.   Sarmatians on Caucasian Steppe. Persian Empire falls to Alexander the Great, 333–323, in Iran, Seleucid Empire following Alexander gradually destroyed by Parni from northern steppe who set up Parthian Empire at its full extent in first century.

C KAZAKHSTAN, ETC.   Sarmatians the most prominent nomads; their early burials near *Chkalov* in fifth to fourth century. After 500 BC Siberian Animal Style develops among Sarmatians under influence from Chorasmia. About 160 BC *Yueh Chi* driven westward through Zungaria press on Sarmatians both there and farther west. Further movements of Sarmatians cross southern Siberia. Successive phases of Sarmatians Animal Style in Siberia over these centuries.

D CENTRAL ASIA, ETC.   After 500 BC, Central Asian Animal Style, having links with styles of Oxus Treasure on edge of Iran. Sarmatian peoples at first dominant in northern Central Asia and in Zungaria. Saka tribes in Aral region allied with Chorasmian cultivators who are in nominal dependence on the Persian Empire. After fall of Achaemenids, Sakas and Chorasmians from late fourth century independent and powerful. Greek kingdom in Bactria independent about 250. Movements arising from the westward flight of the *Yueh Chi* through Zungaria into Central Asia set Sakas moving into Bactria and Parthia in second century to destroy Greek kingdom and pass on into India. *Yueh Chi* in Bactria by *c.* 100; they eventually founded Kushan Empire in first century A D.

E ALTAI, ETC.   Iranians of *Maiemir* and *Pazyryk* cultures in Altai and of *Tagar* culture in Minusinsk give way to Mongoloid peoples, perhaps of Turkish language, who take up mounted nomadism. In first century BC Chinese Han Dynasty makes conquests in Tarim basin.

F FAR EAST   Mongoloid peoples north of China increasingly take up mounted nomadism after Sarmatian example. They form their own cavalry and become dangerous enemies of the Chinese. In second century first nomad empire in Mongolia created by *Hsiung-Nu* who drive *Yueh Chi* westward. Chinese warring states of late Chou period build walls against nomads which are finally made into one system under Ch'in and Han Dynasties. Han Dynasty fights and finally destroys *Hsiung-Nu* power in first century. Later *Ordos* bronzes in last centuries BC. Princely graves of *Noin Ula* from first century BC, containing objects both from China and from eastern borders of Roman Empire.

VI   0–A D 500. Last Phases of Indo-European Period on the Steppes; Dominance of Altaic Nomads from Manchuria to Hungary

A SOUTH RUSSIA   Sarmatians still dominant until third century. Advance body of Huns (Chuni) appear by 150 but do not displace previous nomads. Sarmatian pressure on Danubian province of Roman

Empire. Goths appear from north in third century and conquer South Russia. In late fourth century Huns cross Volga and overcome Goths and Sarmatians in South Russia, and later in Danube valley. Attila becomes King of the Huns in 434 ; creates empire from Caspian to Germany with centre in Hungary under grandees both Hunnish and non-Hunnish. Hunnish golden bows symbolize this. Attila invades Roman territory in the Balkans, Gaul and Italy, but dies in 453.

B CAUCASUS, ETC. Sarmatians dominant until fourth century; make occasional raids into north-west Iran. After fourth century Huns occupy Caucasian Steppe. Parthian rule in Iran overthrown by Sassanids from *Fars* in 229.

C KAZAKHSTAN, ETC. Sarmatians pressed westward by mongoloid peoples gathered into Hunnish horde. Black Huns gather power and move westward, reaching Volga in fourth century. East of the Huns, Turkish peoples begin to move westward, contributing perhaps to the Ephthalite horde.

D CENTRAL ASIA, ETC. Parthian power confronted with Kushans in north-east. Sassanids soon after taking power in Iran break up Kushan power, but are later threatened for a long period by Ephthalite Huns. Turkish peoples by 500 begin to dominate nomad areas of Central Asia, overcoming Ephthalites.

E ALTAI, ETC. Mongoloid peoples dominant, most of them probably speaking Turkish languages. Some of the *Hsiung-Nu* on the Ili river. Chinese influence in Zungaria and Tarim basin continues until fall of Han Dynasty in third century.

F FAR EAST Han Dynasty of China holds back and divides nomads of Mongolia during first and second centuries. *Hsiung-Nu* power destroyed in second century by Han and Sien-Pi. Mongolia later dominated by *Juan-Juan* horde, perhaps the ancestors of the Avars of South Russia and Hungary. *Juan-Juan* overthrown by *Tiu-Kiu* (Turks) in sixth century.

Bibliography

AA   *Artibus Asiae*
AAASH   *Acta Archaeologica Academiae Scientiarum Hungaricae*
BMFEAS *Bulletin of the Museum of Far Eastern Antiquities, Stockholm*
ESA   *Eurasia Septemtrionalis Antiqua*

General

GIMBUTAS, M. *The Prehistory of Eastern Europe* I. American School of Prehistoric Research Bulletin 20, Harvard, 1956

HANČAR, F. Die Skythen als Forschungsproblem, in *Reinecke-Festschrift*, Mainz, 1950, 67–83
Das Pferd in prähistorischer und früher historischer Zeit, Berlin, 1955

JETTMAR, K. Les plus anciennes civilisations d'éleveurs des steppes d'Asia centrale, in *Cahiers d'Histoire Mondiale* I, No. 4, 1954, 760–783

KISELEV, S. V. *Ancient History of Southern Siberia*, Moscow, 1951. In Russian

MINNS, E. H. *Scythians and Greeks*, Cambridge, 1913

MONGAIT, A. *Archaeology in the USSR*, Moscow, 1959

PHILLIPS, E. D. New light on the ancient history of the Eurasian Steppe, in *American Journ. Archaeology*, LXI, 1957, 269–280

RICE, T. T. *The Scythians*, 3rd rev. ed., London, 1961

ROSTOVTZEV, M. *Iranians and Greeks in South Russia*, Oxford, 1922

VERNADSKY, G. *Ancient Russia*, Oxford, 1946

South Russia

PASSEK, T. S. *The Periodization of Tripolyan Settlement*, MIA 10, Moscow, 1949. In Russian
Die ersten Ackerbauern, in *Lebende Vergangenheit*, 1954, 49–70. In a collection of essays by various writers

ROSTOVTZEV, M. *Skythien und der Bosporus* I, Berlin, 1931

Caucasia

HANČAR, F. *Urgeschichte Kaukasiens von den Anfängen bis in die Zeit seiner frühen Metallurgie*, Leipzig, 1937

TALLGREN, A. M. Sur les monuments mégalithiques du Caucase occidental, in *ESA*, IX (1934), 1–45

Trialeti

KUFTIN, B. A. *Archaeological Excavations at Trialeti*, Tiflis, Georgian Academy of Sciences, 1941. In Russian

MINNS, E. H. Trialeti. Review of Kuftin's book in *Antiquity*, XVIII (1943), 129–135

MONGAIT, A. L. *Archaeology in the USSR*, Moscow, 1959, 123–125

SCHAEFFER, C. F. A. In the Wake of the Argo, in *Man*, No. 30 (1944), 43–45

Ananyino

MINNS, E. H. *Scythians and Greeks*, Cambridge, 1913, 257–258

TALLGREN, A. M. L'époque dite d'Ananino dans la Russie Orientale, in *SMYA*, XXXI (1919)

Anatolia

GÖTZE, A. *Kleinasien*, 2nd ed., Berlin, 1957

LLOYD, S. *Early Anatolia*, London, 1956

Iran

GHIRSHMAN, R. *Iran from the Earliest Times to the Islamic Conquest*, London, 1954
Iran : Parthians and Sassanians, London, 1962
Persia from the origins to Alexander the Great, London, 1964

Central Asia

JETTMAR, K. Archäologische Spuren von Indo-Germanen in Zentralasien, in *Paideuma*, v, Heft I (1952), 236–254

Special Problems

HARMATTA, J. Le problème cimmérien, in *Archaeologiai Értesitö*, VII (1946), 79–132
HEINE-GELDERN, R. VON. Das Tocharerproblem und die pontische Wanderung, in *Saeculum*, II (1951), 225–255
JETTMAR, K. Zur Wanderungsgeschichte der Iranier, in *Die Wiener Schule der Völkerkunde, Festschrift zum 25 jährigen Bestand* (1954), 327–348
KRETSCHMER, P. Inder im Kuban, in *Anzeiger der Akademie der Wissenschaften in Wien*, LXXX (1943), 34–42
LEHMANN-HAUPT, C. Article 'Kimmerier', in Pauly-Wissowa *Realencyclopaedi der klassischen Altertumswissenschaft*, XI/1 (1921)
PHILLIPS, E. D. The legend of Aristeas. Fact and fancy in early Greek notions of East Russia, Siberia and Inner Asia, in *AA*, XVIII/2 (1955), 161–177
A further note on Aristeas, in *AA*, XX/2, 3 (1957), 159–162
SULIMIRSKI, T. Scythian antiquities in Western Asia, in *AA*, XVII/3–4 (1954), 282–318
The Cimmerian problem, in *Univ. London Inst. of Archaeology, Bulletin No. 2, 1959* (1960), 45–64

Siberia

GHIRSHMAN, R. Summary of S. V. Kiselev, *Histoire ancienne de la Sibérie* (Moscow, 1949), in *AA*, XIV/2 (1951), 168–189
GRIAZNOV, M. and BOULGAKOV, A. *L'art ancien de l'Altai*, Moscow, 1958
JETTMAR, K. The Karasuk culture and its south-eastern affinities, in *BMFEAS*, 22 (1950), 83–126
The Altai before the Turks, in *BMFEAS*, 23 (1951), 135–223
RUDENKO, S. I. *The Culture of the Peoples of the High Altai in the Scythian Period*, Moscow, 1953. In Russian
Die Schätze der pazyrykschen Kurganen, in *Lebende Vergangenheit* (1954), 129–156
The Culture of the Peoples of the Central Altai in the Scythian Period, Moscow, 1960. In Russian

Nomad Art, The Animal Style, etc.

BOROVKA, G. *Scythian Art*, New York, 1928
GHIRSHMAN, R. Notes Iraniennes IV: le trésor de Sakkez, les origines de l'art mède, et les bronzes de Luristan, in *AA*, XIII (1950), 181–206
GODARD, A. *Les Bronzes de Luristan*, Paris, 1931
Le Trésor de Ziwiyè, Haarlem, 1950
HANČAR, F. Zum Problem des kaukasischen Tierstils, in *Wiener Beiträge zur Kunst- und Kulturgeschichte Asiens*, IX (1934)
Kaukasus-Luristan, in *ESA*, IX (1934), 46–112

MINNS, E. H.   The Art of the Northern Nomads, in *Proc. British Academy*, XXVII (1942), 47–100

ROSTOVTZEV, M.   *The Animal Style in South Russia and China*, Princeton, 1929

The Animal Style

CARTER, D.   *The Symbol of the Beast*, New York, 1957

RUDENKO, S. I.   The Mythological Eagle, the gryphon, the winged lion and the wolf in the Art of the Northern Nomads, in *AA*, XXI (1958), 101–122

TALLGREN, A. M.   Zum Ursprungsgebiet des sogenannten skythischen Tierstils, in *Acta Archaeologica*, IV (1933)

TCHLENOVA, N. L.   Le cerf scythe, in *AA*, XXVI/1 (1963), 27–65

The Scythians and the Greek Settlements on the Russian Coast

MINNS, E. H.   *Scythians and Greeks*, Cambridge, 1913

ROSTOVTZEV, M.   *Iranians and Greeks in South Russia*, Oxford, 1922

RUDENKO, S. I.   *The Culture of the Settlements of the Central Altai in the Scythian Period*, Moscow, 1960. In Russian

SCHULTZ, P. N. and GOLOVKINA, V. A.   Néapolis des Scythes en Ourartou, Néapolis des Scythes Kharezm, in *L'Orient Ancien Illustré*, trans., A. Belkind, Paris, 1954

Central Asia

BERNSHTAM, A. N.   *Historical-Archaeological Sketches of the Central Tien Shan and Pamir-Alai*, Moscow, 1952. In Russian

FRUMKIN, G.   Archaeology in Soviet Central Asia; reports in *Central Asian Review*, X/4 (1962) and following numbers

TOLSTOV, S. P.   *Auf den Spuren der Altchoresmischen Kultur*. Translated from the Russian. Berlin, 1953

The Sarmatians

HARMATTA, J.   *Studies in the History of the Sarmatians*, Budapest, 1950

ROSTOVTZEV, M.   *Iranians and Greeks in South Russia*, Oxford, 1922

SULIMIRSKI, T.   The Forgotten Sarmatians, in *Vanished Civilizations*, ed. Edward Bacon, London, 1963

Sarmatian Art in Siberia

ROSTOVTZEV, M.   *Iranians and Greeks in South Russia*, Oxford, 1922
          The Animal Style in South Russia and China, Princeton, 1929
          The Great Hero of Middle Asia and his Exploits, in *AA*, IV/3 (1930–32), 99–117

RUDENKO, S. I.   The Mythological Eagle, *op. cit.*

SALMONY, A.   *Sino-Siberian Art in the Collection of C. T. Loo*, Paris, 1933
          Sarmatian Gold Work collected by Peter the Great. A series of articles in *Gazette des Beaux Arts* :
  I   Introduction. Vol. 31 (1947), 1–8
  II   The Early Sarmatian Group with all-over cloisonné. Vol. 31 (1947), 9–14
  III   The Early Group with Winged Sockets. Vol. 33 (1948), 321–326
  IV   The Early Sarmatian Group with Embossed Relief. Vol. 35 (1949), 1–10
  V   The Middle Sarmatian Group. Embossed Relief with isolated inlay-cells. Vol. 40 (1952), 85–92

The Sarmatians in South Russia and Eastern Europe

HARMATTA, J. *Studies in the History of the Sarmatians*, Budapest, 1950
SULIMIRSKI, T. The Forgotten Sarmatians, in *Vanished Civilizations*, ed. Edward Bacon, London, 1963

Later Sarmatian Art

FETTICH, N. Archaeologische Beiträge zur Geschichte der Sarmatisch-dakischen Beziehungen, in *AAASH*, III (1953), 127–178
KAPOSHINA, S. I. A Sarmatian Royal Burial at Novocherkassk, in *Antiquity*, XXXVIII (1963), 256–258
MINNS, E. H. *Scythians and Greeks*, Cambridge, 1913
ROSTOVTZEV, M. *Iranians and Greeks in South Russia*, Princeton, 1929

China

KARLGREN, B. Some weapons and tools of the Yin Dynasty, in *BMFEAS*, 17 (1945), 101 ff.
LOEHR, M. Zur Ur- und Vorgeschichte Chinas, in *Saeculum*, III, Heft I (1952), 15–55

Nomad Movements in the East

GHIRSHMAN, R. *Iran*, London, 1954
    Bégram, Recherches Archaeologiques et Historiques sur les Kouchan, Cairo, 1946
    Iran: Parthians and Sassanians, London, 1962
    Persia from the origins to Alexander the Great, London, 1964
LOHUIZEN DE LEEUW, J. E. VAN. *The Scythian Period. An approach to the history, art and palaeography of North India from the 1st Century B.C. to the 3rd Century A.D.*, Leiden, 1949
NARAIN, A. K. *The Indo-Greeks*, Oxford, 1957
TARN, W. W. *The Greeks in Bactria and India*, Cambridge, 1938

The Hsiung Nu and the Huns

ALTHEIM, F. *Geschichte der Hunnen*, Baden-Baden, 1959–62. 5 vols. Vol. I (1959), Vol. IV (1962)
HAMBIS, L. Le Problème des Huns, in *Revue Historique*, CCXX (1958), 249–270
JETTMAR, K. Hunnen und Hsiung Nu. Ein Archaeologisches Problem, in *Archiv für Völkerkunde*, VI–VIII (1951), 166–180
MAENCHEN-HELFEN, O. Huns and Hsiung Nu, in *Byzantion*, XVII (1944–45), 222–243
    The Origin of the Huns, *ibid.*, 244–257

Noin Ula

RUDENKO, S. I. *The Culture of the Huns and the Barrows of Noin Ula*, Moscow, 1962. In Russian
YETTS, W. P. Discoveries of the Kozlov Expedition, in *The Burlington Magazine*, Vol. 48 (1926), 168–183

The Huns

ALTHEIM, F. *Geschichte der Hunnen*, Baden-Baden, 1959–62, 5 vols
HARMATTA, J. The Golden Bow of the Huns, in *AAASH*, I (1951), 107–149
    The Dissolution of the Hun Empire, in *AAASH*, II (1952), 277–304
LASZLO, G. The Significance of the Hun Golden Bow, in *AAASH*, I (1951), 91–104
THOMPSON, E. A. *A History of Attila and the Huns*, Oxford, 1948

List of Illustrations

The author and publishers are grateful to the many official bodies, institutions and individuals mentioned below for their assistance in supplying original illustration material. Illustrations without acknowledgement are from originals in Thames & Hudson's archives.

21 Bronze cloak pin from the Kuban, North Caucasus. Naturhistorisches Museum, Vienna

22 Head of a bronze pin, unprovenanced from Koban. State Hermitage, Leningrad. Drawn by Margaret E. Scott after Rostovtzev

23 Bronze beast from Ananyino. Drawn by Jon Wilsher after Minns

24 Detail of a tombstone from Ananyino with human figure. Drawn by Jon Wilsher after Minns

25 Sword hilt from Ananyino. Drawn by Jon Wilsher after Minns

26 Bronze axe-heads from Koban. Naturhistorisches Museum, Vienna. Drawn by Margaret E. Scott after Hančar

27 Bronze arrowheads; above from Kayakent, Transcaucasia; below from Luristan, unprovenanced. Drawn by Margaret E. Scott and Ian Mackenzie Kerr after Godard

28 Right, bronze dagger from Gandsha, Koban; Left, bronze dagger from Davshanli, Koban, Drawn by Margaret E. Scott after Ginters

29 Bronze axe-heads from the Koban, North Caucasus. Naturhistorisches Museum, Vienna

30 Bronze cheek-piece from Luristan, unprovenanced. Collection David-Weill, Paris. Photo John Freeman

31 Greek terracotta sarcophagus lid from Klazomenai. British Museum. Photo courtesy of the Trustees of the British Museum

32 Pottery model carts. Above and centre, from Kerch, South Russia. Drawn by Margaret E. Scott after Boriskovskii. Below, from Tri-Brata,

Kalmuk Steppe. Drawn by Diana Holmes after Hančar

33 Bronze barbed and socketed arrowheads, from an unprovenanced grave. State Hermitage, Leningrad. Drawn by Margaret E. Scott after Rostovtzev

34 Bronze swords with eared hilt from Osmuškino (left) and Zurovka (right). State Hermitage, Leningrad. Photo John Freeman

35 Copper stag inlaid with electrum and gold from the Royal Cemetery, Alaca Hüyük. Ankara Museum. Photo Stuart Piggott

36 Above left, bronze belt-plate from Kayakent, Transcaucasia. After Virchov. Above right, animal engraving on bronze breast-plate. State Hermitage, Leningrad. After Hančar. Below, bronze belt-plate from Kiev, South Russia. Kiev Museum. After Hančar. Drawn by Margaret E. Scott

37 Bronze axe-head from Lake Van, Armenia. British Museum. Photo courtesy of the Trustees of the British Museum

38 Bronze axe-head, unprovenanced from Luristan. British Museum. Photo courtesy of the Trustees of the British Museum

39 Hittite carved stone slab from Alaca Hüyük. Ankara Museum. Photo Josephine Powell

40 Gold band inlaid with paste from Ziwiye. Metropolitan Museum of Art, New York. Purchase 1958. Funds from various donors

41 Detail of inlaid silver dish from Ziwiye. Archaeological Museum, Teheran. Photo Josephine Powell

42 Gold fish from Vettersfelde. Staatliche Museen zu Berlin

43 Bronze battle axe inlaid with silver, unprovenanced from Uzbekistan. British Museum. Photo Eileen Tweedy

44 Gold stag plaque from Kul Oba, South Russia. Original in the State Hermitage, Leningrad. From an electrotype in the Victoria and Albert Museum. Photo Peter Clayton

45 Gold scabbard from Litoi, South Russia. Original in the State Hermitage, Leningrad. From an electrotype in the Victoria and Albert Museum. Photo Eileen Tweedy

46 Gold pectoral ornament from Ziwiye. Archaeological Museum, Teheran. Photo Josephine Powell

47 Gold eagle-griffin from Ziwiye. Archaeological Museum, Teheran. Photo Josephine Powell

48 Gold plaque with stags and ibexes from Ziwiye. University Museum, Philadelphia. Photo Eileen Tweedy

49 Bronze figure of a stag. Ordos bronze. Victoria and Albert Museum. Photo Victoria and Albert Museum. Crown copyright

50 Bronze figure of a mounted warrior. Ordos bronze. Victoria and Albert Museum. Photo Victoria and Albert Museum. Crown copyright

51 Gold stag plaque from Tapioszentmarton, Hungary. National Museum of Hungary, Budapest

52 Late Chou stag pole terminal, unprovenanced from North China. C. T. Loo Collection, Paris. Photo John Freeman

53 Elk pole terminal. Han Dynasty, unprovenanced from North China. British Museum. Photo Edwin Smith

54 Bronze pole terminal from Ulski Aul, Kuban. State Hermitage, Leningrad

55 Gold ornament from the Seven Brothers Barrow, Kuban. Original in the State Hermitage, Leningrad. From an electrotype in the Victoria and Albert Museum. Photo Eileen Tweedy

56 Gold ornament from the Seven Brothers Barrow, Kuban. State Hermitage, Leningrad

57 Detail of the Great Goddess from the Kelermes mirror. Drawn by Mrs Scott

58 Gold sword sheath from Kul Oba, South Russia. Original in the State Hermitage, Leningrad. From an electrotype in the Victoria and Albert Museum. Photo Eileen Tweedy

59–61 Details of the electrum vase from Kul Oba, South Russia. Original in the State Hermitage, Leningrad. From an electrotype in the Victoria and Albert Museum. Photos Peter Clayton

62 Gold omphalos phiale from Kul Oba, South Russia. Original in the State Hermitage, Leningrad. From an electrotype in the Victoria and Albert Museum. Photo Peter Clayton

63 Gold plaque with dancing women from Kul Oba, South Russia. Original in the State Hermitage, Leningrad. From an electrotype in the Victoria and Albert Museum. Photo Peter Clayton

64 Gold plaque with Pegasus from Kul Oba, South Russia. Original in the State Hermitage, Leningrad. From an electrotype in the Victoria and Albert Museum. Photo Peter Clayton

65 Gold plaque with Scythian horseman from Kul Oba, South Russia. Original in the State Hermitage, Leningrad.

From an electrotype in the Victoria and Albert Museum. Photo Peter Clayton

66 Gold plaque with two Scythians drinking from a single drinking horn from Kul Oba, South Russia. Original in the State Hermitage, Leningrad. From an electrotype in the Victoria and Albert Museum. Photo Peter Clayton

67 Gold bracelet with sphinx's heads terminals from Kul Oba, South Russia. Original in the State Hermitage, Leningrad. From an electrotype in the Victoria and Albert Museum. Photo Peter Clayton

68 Gold bracelet with lions' heads terminals from Kul Oba, South Russia. Original in the State Hermitage, Leningrad. From an electrotype in the Victoria and Albert Museum. Photo Peter Clayton

69, 70 Silver vase inlaid with parcel-gilt scenes of animals fighting from Kul Oba, South Russia. Original in the State Hermitage, Leningrad. From an electrotype in the Victoria and Albert Museum. Photo Peter Clayton

71 Gold stag plaque from Kostromskaya, South Russia. State Hermitage, Leningrad

72 The 'Royal Tomb' with timber mortuary house, Kostromskaya, South Russia. Axonometric reconstruction drawing by Martin E. Weaver

73 Gold panther plaque from Kelermes, South Russia. State Hermitage, Leningrad

74 Ceremonial iron axe with gold cover from Kelermes, South Russia. State Hermitage, Leningrad

75 Hilt of a golden sword from Chertomlyk. State Hermitage, Leningrad

76 Detail of the shoulders of the Chertomlyk vase with Scythians breaking horses. Drawn by Margaret E. Scott

77 The Chertomlyk vase. State Hermitage, Leningrad. Photo courtesy of the German Archaeological Institute

78 Gold plaque with Herakles strangling a lion from Chertomlyk. Original in the State Hermitage, Leningrad. From an electrotype in the Victoria and Albert Museum. Photo Peter Clayton

79 Gold sword scabbard from Chertomlyk. Original in the State Hermitage, Leningrad. From an electrotype in the Victoria and Albert Museum. Photo Eileen Tweedy

80 Gold bowcase from Chertomlyk. Original in the State Hermitage, Leningrad. From an electrotype in the Victoria and Albert Museum. Photo Eileen Tweedy

81, 82 Gold comb, obverse and reverse, from Solokha. State Hermitage, Leningrad

83 Gold brooch from Pantikapaion. City Museum and Art Gallery, Birmingham. Photo Eileen Tweedy

84 Gold funerary mask from Glinishche, near Kerch. Original in the State Hermitage, Leningrad. From an electrotype in the Victoria and Albert Museum. Photo Peter Clayton

85 Gold cap from Ak-Burun. Original in the State Hermitage, Leningrad. From an electrotype in the Victoria and Albert Museum. Photo Peter Clayton

86 Bronze *lebes* from Campania, South Italy. British Museum. Photo Eileen Tweedy

87 Details of tattoo patterns on male corpse from Tomb 2 at Pazyryk. Drawn by Margaret E. Scott after Rudenko

88 Leather reindeer-mask from Tomb 1 at Pazyryk. The State Hermitage, Leningrad

89 Stringed instrument from Tomb 2 at Pazyryk. State Hermitage, Leningrad. Photo Peter Clayton

90 Bronze cauldron and hemp-seeds from Tomb 2 at Pazyryk. State Hermitage, Leningrad. Drawn by Margaret E. Scott after Rudenko

91 Appliqué felt hanging from Tomb 1 at Pazyryk. State Hermitage, Leningrad

92 Woollen pile carpet from Tomb 5 at Pazyryk. State Hermitage, Leningrad

93 Felt hanging from Tomb 5 at Pazyryk. State Hermitage, Leningrad

94 Axonometric plan of Tomb 5 at Pazyryk. Drawn by Martin E. Weaver after Rudenko

95 The burial in Tomb 5 at Pazyryk. Photo courtesy of Dr R. D. Barnett

96 Light chariot in the shaft above the burial chamber in Tomb 5 at Pazyryk. Photo courtesy of Dr R. D. Barnett

97 Detail of a tapestry weave saddle-cloth from Tomb 5 at Pazyryk. State Hermitage, Leningrad. Photo courtesy of Dr R. D. Barnett

98 Appliqué felt hanging from Tomb 5 at Pazyryk. State Hermitage, Leningrad. Photo courtesy of Dr R. D. Barnett

99 Detail of a wooden coffin from Bashadar, Siberia. State Hermitage, Leningrad

100 Gold plaque of a fabulous bird of prey, unprovenanced from Siberia. Original in the State Hermitage, Leningrad. From an electrotype in the Victoria and Albert Museum. Photo Peter Clayton

101 Gilded wooden eagle from a saddle in the second barrow at Bashadar. State Hermitage, Leningrad. Photo courtesy of Artibus Asiae, Switzerland

102 Sarmatian torque ornament. State Hermitage, Leningrad. Photo courtesy of Artibus Asiae, Switzerland

103 Gold armlet from the Oxus Treasure. British Museum. Photo courtesy of the Trustees of the British Museum

104 Sarmatian gold openwork plaque with a tiger and griffin fighting, unprovenanced from Siberia. Original in State Hermitage, Leningrad. From an electrotype in the Victoria and Albert Museum. Photo Eileen Tweedy

105 Sarmatian gold openwork plaque of a boar hunt in wooded country. State Hermitage, Leningrad

106 Sarmatian gold openwork plaque with a warrior resting and horses. Original in the State Hermitage, Leningrad. From an electrotype in the Victoria and Albert Museum. Photo Peter Clayton

107 Sarmatian gold plaque with a wild beast entwined by a serpent. Original in the State Hermitage, Leningrad. From an electrotype in the Victoria and Albert Museum. Photo Peter Clayton

108 Ordos bronze ornament in the shape of a horizontal B. British Museum. Photo John Freeman

109 Ordos bronze ornament with a tiger devouring a ram. British Museum. Photo John Freeman

110 Ordos bronze openwork plaque with two men wrestling in a forest. Victoria and Albert Museum. Photo Victoria and Albert Museum. Crown copyright

111 Detail of Trajan's Column, Rome, with Sarmatian and Roman cavalry. Photo Alinari

112 Sacred stone inscribed with *tamga* signs from Krivoi Rog, Ukraine. Museum of Archaeology, Odessa

113 Gold scent bottle from Novocherkassk. Original in State Hermitage, Leningrad. From an electrotype in the Victoria and Albert Museum. Photo Eileen Tweedy

114 Gold diadem, cup with stag handle, needle-box and perfume-box from Novocherkassk. Originals in State Hermitage, Leningrad. From electrotypes in the Victoria and Albert Museum. Photo Eileen Tweedy

115 Silver gold-embossed *phalera* with a griffin attacking a panther from Novocherkassk. State Hermitage, Leningrad. Photo courtesy of Madame S. I. Kaposhina

116 Silver bowl with satirical harvest scene in the tondo from Novocherkassk. State Hermitage, Leningrad. Photo courtesy of Madame S. I. Kaposhina

117 Silver bowl with Nereid and hippocamp from Novocherkassk. State Hermitage, Leningrad. Photo courtesy of Madame S. I. Kaposhina

118 Silver bowl with Cupid and Psyche from Novocherkassk. State Hermitage, Leningrad. Photo courtesy of Madame S. I. Kaposhina

119 Bronze cauldron from Novocherkassk. State Hermitage, Leningrad. Photo courtesy of Madame S. I. Kaposhina

120 Gold ornament with a beheading scene from the Zubov barrow, near Anapa. Feron-Stoclet Collection, Brussels

121 Gold ornament with Scythian holding a severed head from Kurdzhips barrow. State Hermitage, Leningrad

122 Silver-gilt *phalera* from the shores of the Black Sea. Cabinet des Médailles, Paris

123 Bronze gilt fibula with a figure brandishing the severed head of an enemy from Maikop. University Museum of the University of Philadelphia

124 Silver-gilt *phalera* with a man in a quilted jacket from Herastrau, Rumania. National Antiquities Museum, Rumania. Photo courtesy of the Director

125 *Phalera* with Great Goddess, her hair in heavy plaits, from Galiche, Bulgaria. National Museum, Sofia. Photo courtesy of the Director

126 *Phalera* with decorative lozenge pattern and central rosette from Galiche, Bulgaria. National Museum, Sofia. Photo courtesy of the Director

127 Decorated *phalera* from Galiche, Bulgaria. National Museum, Sofia. Photo courtesy of the Director

128 *Phalera* with horseman and sacred eagle from Surcea. Regional Museum of Sf. Gheorghe, Rumania. Photo courtesy of the Director

129 *Phalera* with Sarmatian rider in a long cloak with a high collar from Galiche, Bulgaria. National Museum, Sofia. Photo courtesy of the Director

Index

Numbers in italics refer to illustrations